**New Directions for
Adult and Continuing
Education**

Susan Imel
Jovita M. Ross-Gordon
COEDITORS-IN-CHIEF

Challenging Ableism, Understanding Disability, Including Adults with Disabilities in Workplaces and Learning Spaces

Tonette S. Rocco
EDITOR

Number 132 • Winter 2011
Jossey-Bass
San Francisco

CHALLENGING ABLEISM, UNDERSTANDING DISABILITY, INCLUDING ADULTS WITH DISABILITIES IN WORKPLACES AND LEARNING SPACES
Tonette S. Rocco (ed.)
New Directions for Adult and Continuing Education, no. 132
Susan Imel, Jovita M. Ross-Gordon, Coeditors-in-Chief

Microfilm copies of issues and articles are available in 16mm and 35mm, as well as microfiche in 105mm, through University Microfilms Inc., 300 North Zeeb Road, Ann Arbor, Michigan 48106-1346.

NEW DIRECTIONS FOR ADULT AND CONTINUING EDUCATION (ISSN 1052-2891, electronic ISSN 1536-0717) is part of The Jossey-Bass Higher and Adult Education Series and is published quarterly by Wiley Subscription Services, Inc., A Wiley Company, at Jossey-Bass, One Montgomery Street, Suite 1200, San Francisco, CA 94104-4594. Periodicals Postage Paid at San Francisco, California, and at additional mailing offices. POSTMASTER: Send address changes to New Directions for Adult and Continuing Education, Jossey-Bass, One Montgomery Street, Suite 1200, San Francisco, CA 94104-4594

New Directions for Adult and Continuing Education is indexed in CIJE: Current Index to Journals in Education (ERIC); Contents Pages in Education (T&F); ERIC Database (Education Resources Information Center); Higher Education Abstracts (Claremont Graduate University); and Sociological Abstracts (CSA/CIG).

SUBSCRIPTIONS for print and electronic in the U.S. cost $98.00 for individuals and $316.00 for institutions, agencies, and libraries.

EDITORIAL CORRESPONDENCE should be sent to the Coeditors-in-Chief, Susan Imel, ERIC/ACVE, 1900 Kenny Road, Columbus, Ohio 43210-1090, e-mail: imel.l@osu.edu; or Jovita M. Ross-Gordon, Southwest Texas State University, EAPS Dept., 601 University Drive, San Marcos, TX 78666.

Cover photograph by Jack Hollingsworth@Photodisc

www.josseybass.com

CONTENTS

Editor's Notes

At present, there is no issue of diversity, privilege, or human rights in the field of adult education that has been given less attention than disability. In the U.S. adult education literature, looking back as far as the Knowles 1960 edition of the *Handbook of Adult Education*, disability was included in two handbooks (see Klugerman, 1989; Rocco and Fornes, 2010). From 1984 to 2010, ten articles were published on disability in *Adult Education Quarterly*. Five of these are on issues surrounding HIV/AIDS; the others are on diabetes and cardiac patient education. An issue of *Adult Learning* (2001) was dedicated to adults with disabilities, and a few books have been published (Gadbow and DuBois, 1998; Ross-Gordon, 1989; Jordan, 1996). While not complete, this brief listing illustrates the lack of attention paid to disability issues by adult education. We hope that this sourcebook brings attention to disability and helps the field broaden its view of disability from a medical or economic concern to a social justice concern.

Disability affects adults across the life span, at work, and while seeking further education. This sourcebook examines practical and research aspects of disability and presents reflections on experience with disability as a person with a disability, a service provider, parent, or teacher. The first three chapters situate disability as a political and social justice concern. In Chapter 1, Tonette S. Rocco and Antonio Delgado provide an overview on disability by presenting concepts and theories from disability studies useful for a critical examination of disability in adult education. In Chapter 2, Margaret A. McLean examines the role of contact and relationship in changing ableist beliefs and concepts about disability. In Chapter 3, Kelly M. Munger and Donna M. Mertens explore the philosophical and theoretical frameworks that are useful for conducting research with people with disabilities that supports social change and enhances human rights.

The next three chapters provide personal insights into disability from the perspectives of those with disabilities, questioning disability classifications, and parents of children with disabilities. In Chapter 4, Stephen Brookfield relates his personal learning journey to discover how best to cope with clinical depression. In Chapter 5, Wayland Walker queries how one type of human difference—alterity, the experience of multiple distinct consciousnesses, or "alters," by one person—is pathologized in American culture. In Chapter 6, Thomas G. Reio, Jr., and Sandra L. Fornes explore their learning and adaptation after diagnosis of their children's disability and offer suggestions for navigating the resources available to parents.

The last four chapters take a pragmatic stance to look at the experiences of disabled veterans, adults with learning disabilities, and the law. In Chapter 7, Fariba Ostovary and Janet Dapprich present an overview of

New Directions for Adult and Continuing Education, no. 132, Winter 2011 © 2011 Wiley Periodicals, Inc.
Published online in Wiley Online Library (wileyonlinelibrary.com) • DOI: 10.1002/ace.425

issues related to transitioning from the military to the civilian workplace and learning environments of disabled military servicemen/women. Specific emphasis is placed on the unique experiences of veterans who became disabled while serving in Operation Enduring Freedom/Operation Iraqi Freedom. In Chapter 8, Alisa Belzer and Jovita Ross-Gordon discuss the current policy emphasis on evidence-based instruction by examining two recent publications on adult learning disabilities that view learning disabilities as cognitive disorders and fail to attend to adult learning theory and the importance of a sociocultural perspective. In Chapter 9, Lorenzo Bowman reviews the impact of amendments and regulations that have updated the Americans with Disabilities Act in its twentieth year with an emphasis on employment and adult and higher education. Finally, in Chapter 10, Tonette S. Rocco describes the major themes discussed in the text regarding disability and presents takeaways for adult education.

Tonette S. Rocco
Editor

References

Gadbow, N. F., and DuBois, D. A. *Adult Learners with Special Needs: Strategies and Resources for Postsecondary Education and Workplace Training*. Melbourne, Fla.: Krieger Publishing, 1998.

Klugerman, P. B. "Developmentally Disabled Adult Learners." In S. Merriam and P. Cunningham (eds.), *Handbook of Adult and Continuing Education*. San Francisco: Jossey-Bass, 1989.

Jordan, D. *Teaching Adults with Learning Disabilities*. Malabar, Fla.: Krieger Publishing, 1996.

Rocco, T., and Fornes, S. "Perspectives on Disability in Adult and Continuing Education." In A. Rose, C. Kasworm, and J. Ross-Gordon (eds.), *The Handbook of Adult and Continuing Education*. Thousand Oaks: Sage, 2010.

Ross-Gordon, J. M. *Adults with Learning Disabilities: An Overview for the Adult Educator*. (Information Series No. 337). Columbus, OH: ERIC Clearinghouse on Adult, Career, and Vocational Education, 1989. (ERIC No. ED315 664.)

TONETTE S. ROCCO *is associate professor and graduate program director, Adult Education and Human Resource Development, and director of the Office of Academic Writing and Publication Support, Florida International University, Miami, Florida.*

New Directions for Adult and Continuing Education • DOI: 10.1002/ace

1

Adult educators discuss disability as an organizing variable, rarely troubling the concept of disability as an identity marker by examining its social construction.

Shifting Lenses: A Critical Examination of Disability in Adult Education

Tonette S. Rocco, Antonio Delgado

Medical advances increase the number of people with disabilities who have conditions that might have caused death just years before. Environmental degradation through the rapid progression of business, industry, and technology contribute to increases in chronic disease. War, terrorism, and police actions are major causes of impairment (Priestley, 2001). In fact, of the 21.9 million veterans in the United States in 2009, one in four had a disability (U.S. Census Bureau, 2010). In the year 2008, an estimated 12.1 percent of the noninstitutionalized population in the United States reported a disability (Erickson, Lee, and von Schrader, 2010). Due to medical advances at home and on the battlefield, growing numbers of the "well" disabled are demanding access to opportunities for education and training, work, and leisure.

The purpose of this chapter is to critique the ways adult educators discuss disability. To enhance the discourse on disability from a critical perspective, we present concepts and theories from disability studies useful for a critical examination of disability in adult education. Disability should be an important concern for adult education and adult educators for at least three reasons.

1. The process of becoming disabled provides opportunities for the person with the disability and his or her family to learn about the disability.
2. Increasing numbers of students with disabilities enroll in formal adult and higher education programs.

NEW DIRECTIONS FOR ADULT AND CONTINUING EDUCATION, no. 132, Winter 2011 © 2011 Wiley Periodicals, Inc.
Published online in Wiley Online Library (wileyonlinelibrary.com) • DOI: 10.1002/ace.426

3. Disability is an identity marker that diminishes opportunities for work, education, and leisure.

We provide a brief discussion of the state of research and thinking on disability in adult education. Next, we present four concepts from disability studies: disability as social construction, the comprehensive theory of disability oppression (Charlton, 1998), critical disability theory (Rocco, 2005), and critical theory of "dis-citizenship" (Devlin and Pothier, 2006). We conclude the chapter by making connections between disability studies and adult education.

Disability in Adult Education

Adult educators conduct research based on specific impairment, such as HIV/AIDS (Courtenay, Merriam, and Reeves, 1998), learning disabilities (Jordan, 1996; Ross-Gordon, 1989), Deaf/Hard of Hearing. (Clark, 2002), cancer (Rager, 2003), and heart disease (Wise, Yun, and Shaw, 2000). Adult educators write about disability experiences as they relate to transformational learning around HIV/AIDS (Courtenay, Merriam, and Reeves, 1998), specialized health education programs (Wise, Yun, and Shaw, 2000), literacy and adult basic education (learning disabilities) (Jordan, 1996; Ross-Gordon, 1989), and education and workplace accommodations (Gadbow and DuBois, 1998). Often this research is from the perspective of medical or functional models. Few adult educators situate research on disability in critical theory when writing on and examining disability (Hahn, 1988).

We know race, gender, and class are socially constructed, but adult educators the field do not see disability as a constructed state; rather, disability is seen as an unfortunate condition, and the person with a disability is viewed as a poor unfortunate victim (Rocco, 2005). Adult educators rarely see or acknowledge the fluid boundaries of disability and how they intersect our other identities. Rather, they discuss disability as an organizing variable, rarely troubling the concept of disability as an identity marker by examining its social construction. For instance, Archie-Booker, Cervero, and Langone (1999) examined the politics of planning culturally relevant AIDS prevention education. The political and cultural aspects of the programs were not centered on AIDS as disability and as socially and politically constructed but rather on how relevant the education was to African American women. Certainly, a necessary step toward being inclusive is to acknowledge/honor this one aspect of identity, the African American female. However, ignoring the AIDS/HIV positive identity perpetuates the binary categorization and reductionism that underlie the American economic, legal, and political system (Delgado and Stefanic, 2001) and supports the dominant power structure.

Boshier (1991) warned that "the way this disease [AIDS] is discussed can influence relationships to it and our ability to learn or teach about it"

New Directions for Adult and Continuing Education • DOI: 10.1002/ace

(p. 15) and impacts our students who have this additional identity marker. In 1990, he critiqued the functionalist, medical approach of AIDS education. What is striking about Boshier's series of papers (1990; 1991; 1993) is that the emergent notion of the sociopolitical construction of disability and disease was not taken up again until 2000 (Egan, 2000; Gorman, 2000).

As of 2011, the adult education work around disability issues has just barely broken ground on other important issues, ranging from the individual person to the social context. Some of the adult education literature involving disability issues has explored the way individuals make new meaning regarding their identity and environment as a result of their disability status (Baumgartner, 2002, 2005; Baumgartner and David, 2009; Courtenay, Merriam, and Reeves 1998; Courtenay, Merriam, Reeves, and Baumgartner, 2000), learning experiences parenting a child with a disability (Hill, 2001), or the interpersonal dynamics involving disability disclosure (Rocco, 2001). Other work has explored teaching strategies (Covington, 2004; Gadbow 2001, 2002; Haddad, 1995; Summers, 2008) to inform practice in formal adult and higher education programs. Last, examining the structural relationships of power (Gorman, 2000) and education as a mechanism for social change (Beziat, 1990) is a starting point for adult educators to engage in research that will further uncover discrimination of disabled people resulting in the diminished opportunity for work, education, and leisure.

Concepts from Disability Studies

The field of disability studies provides a location for the deconstruction of disability and an examination of the cultural, political, and social ramifications of disability in society (Rocco and Fornes, 2010). As an interdisciplinary field, it provides a location for theorizing and considering disability beyond the medical and economic perspectives.

Disability as a Social Construct. The power of naming is personal and political; often it is the first battleground for minority groups seeking civil rights (Zola, 1993). Oliver (1990) points out that definitions are important for three reasons:

1. They are important because "human beings give meanings to objects in the social world" (p. 2). These meanings influence our behavior toward the objects.
2. Definitions fulfill our need to identify and classify.
3. In order for society to ameliorate or deal with a social problem, "nothing more or less than a fundamental redefinition of the problem [is] necessary" (p. 3).

For instance, the earlier label "handicapped" has evolved to "people with disabilities" to "disabled people" by those in the disability rights movement.

New Directions for Adult and Continuing Education • DOI: 10.1002/ace

Gleeson (1999) reasons: "The term 'disabled people' serves a political purpose by foregrounding the oppression—in other words, the socially imposed disability—that bears down upon impaired people" (p. 9). Priestly (2001) explains that the term "disabled people" emphasizes the structural location of disability as "a form of social oppression residing outside the person" (p. xvii).

The definition of disability is contested terrain by people with specific disabilities (such as the Deaf) and their organizations and by disability studies scholars (Thomas, 2003), who use two meanings: "disability as restricted activity" (Thomas, 2003, p. 2) and disability as a form of social oppression (Oliver, 1990, 1996). Disability as restricted activity "corresponds to a normative meaning of disability in our culture: that is—that disability is about not being able to do things" (Thomas, 2003, p. 3). Restricted activity, disabling environments, and the invisibility of disability are by-products of ableism.

Ableism is "a network of beliefs, processes and practices that produces a particular kind of self and body (the corporeal standard) that is projected as the perfect, species-typical and therefore essential and fully human. Disability then, is cast as a diminished state of being human" (Campbell, 2001, p. 44). Ableism also includes paternalistic elements of sympathy, economic subordination, and treating adults like children who are "assumed to be helpless, dependent, asexual, economically unproductive, physically limited, emotionally immature, and acceptable only when they are unobtrusive" so that able-bodied people can "act as the protectors, guides, leaders, role models, and intermediaries for disabled individuals" (Hahn, 1986, p. 130).

Disability is socially constructed, and it is the person-created environment that is disabling, not the physical, cognitive, or mental variation that an individual experiences (Hahn, 1988). The environment becomes disabling when spaces are created without regard to the needs of people with disabilities. Asch (2001) proposes a human variation approach, suggesting that instead of maintaining the dichotomy—disabled or not disabled—we should determine how to modify the environment, not the individual.

People with disabilities have a unique voice emerging from particular individual and group experiences. These experiences are as rich and varied as are the disabilities and their manifestations. Disability should be recognized with true minority group status instead of viewed as an individual anomaly. Discrimination and oppression against people with disabilities is so ordinary that it is invisible.

Comprehensive Theory of Disability Oppression. The comprehensive theory of disability oppression emerged as Charlton (1998) collected oral histories and reflected on the nature of disability and oppression around the world. The theory is explained through four tenets:

1. Political economy
2. Culture(s) and belief systems

3. (False) consciousness and alienation
4. Power and ideology

Political economy is informed by where and how individuals "are incorporated into a world system dominated by the few that control the means of production and force" (Charlton, 1998, p. 23). This world system keeps people with disabilities poor, unemployed, or underemployed, and sustains an industry that benefits from the oppression of people with disabilities. Disabled people are decidedly outcasts, surplus labor, and declassed. Under ordinary circumstances, disabled people will not be used to produce, exchange, and distribute political and economic goods and services.

Culture and belief systems support the attitude that disability is abnormal and pitiful. For instance, "ideas and beliefs are informed by and in cultures, [which] are partial expressions of a world in which the dualities of domination/subordination, superiority/inferiority, normality/abnormality are relentlessly reinforced and legitimized" (Charlton, 1998, p. 26).

False consciousness and alienation is internalizing the dominant view of disability by believing that one is not able to perform, is less capable, and is less worthy. Alienation becomes self-annihilation when it prevents disabled people from "knowing their real selves, their real needs, and their real capabilities" (Charlton, 1998, p. 27) and recognizing their options. Authentic consciousness informs being when an individual becomes critically aware of the social conditions, opportunities, and oppressive forces that exist.

The dominant group uses power and ideology to maintain order through the capacity to cause events and to control resources (Clegg, 1989). Education is useful in maintaining the dominant power structure through "teaching acquiescence to power structures" (Charlton, 1998, p. 31). Educational institutions further support oppression by labeling and separating disabled students from nondisabled students through separate structures (entry points, classrooms) and specially designed curricula and through "testing and evaluation biased toward the functional needs of the dominant culture" (Charlton, 1998, p. 33).

Critical Disability Theory. In 2005, Rocco presented an initial conceptualization of critical disability theory that emerged from her reading of the disability studies and the critical race theory literature. The six principles that explain the theory are:

1. Disabled people have a unique voice and complex experience.
2. Disability should be viewed as part of a continuum of human variation (Asch, 2001).
3. Disability is socially constructed (Oliver, 1990; 1996).
4. Ableism is invisible.
5. Disabled people have a right to self-determination (Gorman, 2000).

New Directions for Adult and Continuing Education • DOI: 10.1002/ace

6. The commodification of labor and disability business (the industry that exists to care for people with disabilities such as nursing homes, step down facilities, and so on) combine to maintain a system of poverty and isolation among people with disabilities (Albrecht, 1992).

Devlin and Pothier (2006) introduced a critical theory of dis-citizenship that includes the following principles. First, people with disabilities experience "unequal citizenship" (p. 1). Citizenship is about more than individual status, it is "a practice that locates individuals in the larger community" (pp. 1–2) and includes access to meaningful work and the full spectrum of society. Second are issues involving language, definitions, and voice. Devlin and Pothier critique the language used to describe a person with "a disability" by pointing out that we do not say person with "a gender" or "a race." Next they ask what constitutes a disability. Since disability has no essential nature and is socially constructed, they suggest context determines whether a person is disabled. Third, political insights on powerlessness and context (physical locations, roles and responsibilities, social values, institutional priorities, and political will) must be used to interrogate the hierarchy of difference, liberalism, and "deep structural assumptions such as the narrative of progress" (p. 9). Fourth, a primary goal is to move toward a barrier-free society. Applying these tenets and principles to research in adult education and disability will unmask systemic oppression and move adult educators away from the assumption that disability is a private, personal, and individual concern.

Making Connections

Disability is rarely explored as a social construct, a political concern, or an experience that warrants a theoretical framework in adult education. Since we rarely consider disability as an issue of power or think of ourselves as teaching or recruiting students with disabilities, it may not seem like an important issue. However, 11 percent of U.S. postsecondary students self-reported as having disabilities in 2003–2004, equal to the percentage of African Americans enrolled in the same year (U.S. Department of Education, 2006), and since that time, these numbers have grown. A large number of these students have invisible disabilities, such as learning disabilities, depression, traumatic brain injury, or back injuries. Some are entering college to study a field that does not require physical labor or skills diminished or altered by the disability.

Research on the experience of disability should be conducted that facilitates personal liberation, recognizes individual rights, and attends to the agenda of people with disabilities (Moore, Beazley, and Maelzer, 1998). This agenda includes access to and participation in education, meaningful work, and participation in the civic and social life of the community. Just as some in adult education have invited and made space for African American and feminist scholars, we need to make space for disability so that students feel comfortable with exploring research agendas centered on disability and adult education.

Novice scholars in adult education have few mentors with whom to discuss disability as a social construct or a political designation. However, adult educators investigate issues of power and privilege in terms of race, gender, and sexual orientation without being members of these groups (Brooks and Edwards, 1997; Johnson-Bailey and Cervero, 1998; Tisdell and Taylor, 1995). Can an able-bodied person conduct research that contributes to our knowledge of disability as a sociopolitical construct? Disability theorists maintain the ability to conduct research is in how the questions are framed (Linton, 1998). Questions about disability could interrogate ableism, voice, experience, and other manifestations of power and privilege in adult education.

When discussing multicultural issues, we rarely concede that disabled people constitute a minority group with shared experiences of discrimination and few opportunities for education and employment (Ross-Gordon, 1991). The study of disability and institutional and structural barriers to educational access should not be seen in isolation from the work already being done on power and privilege in adult education. Instead, disability should be integrated into the stream of research on power and privilege. While disability scholars have "fought hard to get disability included in the race-class-gender triad" (Davis, 2001, p. 535), inclusion happens only in the disability studies literature, not in the adult education literature. In order to theorize disability as a public issue, it must become as visible as the race-class-gender triad.

References

Albrecht, G. L. *The Disability Business: Rehabilitation in America*. Sage Library of Social Research, no. 190. Newbury Park, Calif.: Sage, 1992.

Archie-Booker, D. E., Cervero, R. M., and Langone, C. A. "The Politics of Planning Culturally Relevant AIDS Prevention Education for African-American Women." *Adult Education Quarterly*, 1999, 49, 163–175.

Asch, A. "Critical Race Theory, Feminism, and Disability: Reflections on Social Justice and Personal Identity." *Ohio State Law Journal*, 2001, 62(1) 391–423.

Baumgartner, L. M. "Living and Learning with HIV/AIDS: Transformational Tales Continued." *Adult Education Quarterly*, 2002, 53(1), 44–59.

Baumgartner, L. M. "HIV-Positive Adults' Meaning Making over Time." In J. Egan, ed., *HIV/AIDS Sourcebook* (pp. 11–20). New Directions for Adult and Continuing Education, no. 105. San Francisco: Jossey Bass, 2005.

Baumgartner, L. M., and David, K. N. "PoZitively Transformative: The Transformative Learning of People Living with HIV." *Proceedings of the 50th Annual Adult Education Research Conference*. Louisville, Ky.: National-Louis University, 2009.

Beziat, C. "Educating America's Last Minority: Adult Education's Role in the Americans with Disabilities Act." *Adult Learning*, 1990, 2(2), 21–23.

Boshier, R. "Ideological and Epistemological Foundations of Education About AIDS." *Proceedings of the 31st Annual Adult Education Research Conference*. Athens: University of Georgia, 1990.

Boshier, R. "Popular Discourse Concerning Women and AIDS." *Proceedings of the 32nd Annual Adult Education Research Conference*. Norman: University of Oklahoma, 1991.

Boshier, R. W. "Constructing HIV and Magic Johnson: Discourse, Education and Power." *Proceedings of the 34th Annual Adult Education Research*. State College: Pennsylvania State University, 1993.

Brooks, A. K., and Edwards, K. A. "Narratives of Women's Sexual Identity Development: A Collaborative Inquiry with Implications for Rewriting Transformative Learning Theory." *Proceedings of the 38th Annual Adult Education Research Conference*. Stillwater: Oklahoma State University, 1997.

Campbell, F. K. "Inciting Legal Fictions: Disability's Date with Ontology and the Ableist Body of the Law." *Griffith Law Review*, 2001, *10*, 42–62.

Charlton, J. I. *Nothing About Us Without Us: Disability Oppression and Empowerment*. Berkeley: University of California Press, 1998.

Clark, M. "Do You Hear What I See: Learning Experiences of Black Men Who Are Deaf or Hard of Hearing." *Proceedings of the 43rd Annual Adult Education Research Conference*. Raleigh: North Carolina State University, 2002.

Clegg, S. R. *Frameworks of Power*. London: Sage, 1989.

Courtenay, B. C., Merriam, S. B., and Reeves, P. M. "The Centrality of Meaning-Making in Transformational Learning: How HIV-Positive Adults Make Sense of Their Lives." *Adult Education Quarterly*, 1998, *48*(2), 65–84.

Courtenay, B. C., Merriam, S., Reeves, P., and Baumgartner, L. "Perspective Transformation Over Time: A 2-Year Follow-Up Study of HIV-Positive Adults." *Adult Education Quarterly*, 2000, *50*(2), 102–119.

Covington, L. E. "Moving Beyond the Limits of Learning: Implications of Learning Disabilities for Adult Education." *Adult Basic Education*, 2004, *14*(2), 90–103.

Davis, L. J. "Identity Politics, Disability, and Culture." In G. L. Albrecht, K. D. Seelman, and M. Bury (eds.), *Handbook of Disability Studies*. Thousand Oaks, Calif.: Sage, 2001.

Delgado, R., and Stefanic, J. *Critical Race Theory: An Introduction*. New York: New York University Press, 2001.

Devlin, R., and Pothier, D. "Introduction: Toward a Critical Theory of Dis-Citizenship." In D. Pothier and R. Devlin (eds.), *Critical Disability Theory: Essays in Philosophy, Politics, Policy, and Law*. Vancouver: University of British Columbia Press, 2006.

Egan, J. "Interdictions and Benedictions—AIDS Prevention Discourses in Vancouver Canada." *Proceedings of the 41st Annual Adult Education Research Conference*. Vancouver: University of British Columbia, 2000.

Erickson, W., Lee, C., and von Schrader, S. "Disability Statistics from the 2008 American Community Survey (ACS)." Ithaca, N.Y.: Cornell University Rehabilitation Research and Training Center on Disability Demographics and Statistics, 2010. www.disabilitystatistics.org.

Gadbow, N. F. "Teaching Strategies That Help Learners with Different Needs." *Adult Learning*, 2001, *12*(2), 19–21.

Gadbow, N. F. "Teaching All Learners as If They Are Special." *New Directions for Adult and Continuing Education*, 2002, *93*, 51–61.

Gadbow, N. F., and DuBois, D. A. *Adult Learners with Special Needs: Strategies and Resources for Postsecondary Education and Workplace Training*. Malabar, Fla.: Krieger Publishing, 1998.

Gleeson, B. *Geographies of Disability*. London: Routledge, 1999.

Gorman, R. "Research That Hurts or Research that Helps? A Critical Framework for Adult Education Inquiry and People with Intellectual Disabilities." *Proceedings of the*

41st Annual Adult Education Research Conference. Vancouver: University of British Columbia, 2000.

Haddad, P. J. "Teaching the Learning-Disabled Adult." *Adult Learning,* 1995, 6(4), 9.

Hahn, H. "The Politics of Physical Differences: Disability and Discrimination." *Journal of Social Issues,* 1988, 44(1), 39–47.

Hahn, H. "Public Support for Rehabilitation Programmes: The Analysis of U.S. Disability Policy." *Disability, Handicap and Society,* 1986, 1(2), 121–137.

Hill, L. H. "My Child Has a Learning Disability. Now What?" *Adult Learning,* 2001, 12(2), 24—25.

Johnson-Bailey, J., and Cervero, R. M. "Positionality: Whiteness as a Social Construct That Drives Classroom Dynamics." *Proceedings of the 39th Annual Adult Education Research Conference.* San Antonio, Tex.: University of the Incarnate Word, 1998.

Jordan, D. *Teaching Adults with Learning Disabilities.* Malabar, Fla.: Krieger Publishing, 1996.

Linton, S. *Claiming Disability: Knowledge and Identity.* New York: New York University Press, 1998.

Moore, M., Beazley, S., and Maelzer, J. *Researching Disability Issues.* Buckingham, U.K.: Open University Press, 1998.

Oliver, M. *The Politics of Disablement.* New York: St. Martin's Press, 1990.

Oliver, M. *Understanding Disability: From Theory to Practice.* New York: St. Martin's Press, 1996.

Priestly, M. "A Brief Note on Terminology." In M. Priestly (ed.), *Disability and the Life Course: Global Perspectives.* Cambridge, U.K.: Cambridge University Press, 2001.

Rager, K. B. "The Self-Directed Learning of Women with Breast Cancer." *Adult Education Quarterly,* 2003, 53(4), 277–293.

Rocco, T. S. "Helping Adult Educators Understand Disability Disclosure." *Adult Learning,* 2001, 12(2), 10–12.

Rocco, T. S. "From Disability Studies to Critical Race Theory: Working Towards Critical Disability Theory." *Proceedings of the 46th Annual Adult Education Research Conference.* Athens: University of Georgia, 2005.

Rocco, T., and Fornes, S. "Perspectives on Disability in Adult and Continuing Education." In A. Rose, C. Kasworm, and J. Ross-Gordon (eds.), *The Handbook of Adult and Continuing Education.* Thousand Oaks, Calif.: Sage, 2010.

Ross-Gordon, J. *Adults with Learning Disabilities: An Overview for the Adult Educator.* (Information Series no. 337). Columbus, Ohio: ERIC Clearinghouse on Adult, Career, and Vocational Education, Center on Education and Training for Employment, The Ohio State University, 1989. (ERIC No. Ed 315 664.)

Ross-Gordon, J. "Needed: A Multicultural Perspective for Adult Education Research." *Adult Education Quarterly,* 1991, 42(1), 1–16.

Summers, T. "Teaching Adults with Disabilities in the Postsecondary Setting: Examining the Experiences of Faculty Members." *Proceedings of the 49th Annual Adult Education Research Conference.* St. Louis: University of Missouri-St. Louis, 2008.

Thomas, C. "Defining a Theoretical Agenda for Disability Studies." Keynote address, inaugural conference of the Disabilities Studies Association. Lancaster, U.K.: University of Lancaster, 2003.

Tisdell, E., and Taylor, E. W. "Out of the Closet: Lesbian and Gay Adult Educators and Sexual Orientation Issues in the University Learning Environment." *Proceedings of the 36th Annual Adult Education Research Conference.* Edmonton: University of Alberta, 1995.

U.S. Census Bureau. "Facts for Features: Veterans Day 2010: Nov. 11." Washington, D.C.: Bureau of the Census, 2010. www.census.gov/newsroom/releases/pdf/cb10ff-21_veteransday.pdf.

U.S. Department of Education. "Profile of Undergraduates in U.S. Postsecondary Education Institutions: 2003–04." Washington, D.C.: National Center for Education Statistics, 2006.

Wise, M., Yun, G. W., and Shaw, B. "Mapping Use of Self-Directed On-line Heart Disease Education Program onto Health Learning Outcomes: A Study of Post Heart Attack Learners." *Proceedings of the 41st Annual Adult Education Research Conference.* Vancouver: University of British Columbia, 2000.

Zola, I. "Self, Identity and the Naming Question: Reflections on the Language of Disability." In M. Nagler (ed.), *Perspectives on Disability*. Palo Alto, Calif.: Health Markets Research, 1993.

TONETTE S. ROCCO is associate professor and graduate program director, Adult Education and Human Resource Development, Florida International University, Miami, Florida.

ANTONIO DELGADO is a doctoral candidate in adult education and human resource development, Florida International University, Miami, Florida.

New Directions for Adult and Continuing Education • DOI: 10.1002/ace

2

Adult education is one context where ableist notions may persist unrecognized and unchallenged as these understandings have become institutionalized in the beliefs, language, and practices of nondisabled people

Getting to Know You: The Prospect of Challenging Ableism Through Adult Learning

Margaret A. McLean

Ableism is discrimination on the grounds that being able bodied is the normal and superior human condition. In contrast, being "disabled" is linked to ill health, incapacity, and dependence. These understandings become institutionalized in the beliefs, language, and practices of nondisabled people and create barriers to equitable social participation for many disabled people. Able-bodied people are often unaware of the constraining impact of disability. For that reason, they are likely to assume that the circumstances of their able-bodied world are universal (Komesaroff and McLean, 2006). Adult education is one context where ableist notions may persist unrecognized and unchallenged as these understandings have become institutionalized in the beliefs, language, and practices of nondisabled people. The fact that most teachers and learners currently are able-bodied individuals may also complicate and obscure ableist prejudice.

The purpose of this chapter is to suggest the potential of contact and relationship of able-bodied people with disabled people to lead adult learners to begin to identify, confront, and change ableist views of disability. Further, the aim of the chapter is to consider the implications of contact for initial and ongoing professional development. When a hegemonic understanding, such as the superiority of the able-bodied condition, is intimately connected to a professional role, the risks involved in challenging such an understanding include the possibility of changing a valued professional identity. This is because when able-bodied persons get to know disabled people, the basis of their previously unquestioned notions of ability and disability

NEW DIRECTIONS FOR ADULT AND CONTINUING EDUCATION, no. 132, Winter 2011 © 2011 Wiley Periodicals, Inc.
Published online in Wiley Online Library (wileyonlinelibrary.com) • DOI: 10.1002/ace.427

and normality and abnormality may be challenged. In some circumstances, however, the disparity between old and new understandings may be insufficient to promote change and instead serve to reaffirm currently held ableist notions. In choosing to avoid the discomfort such change brings, professionals may remain in the state of not knowing "what they do does" for the recipients of their services (Foucault, 1980, cited in Ware, 2002, p. 145).

Nature and Role of Knowledge and Beliefs

Knowledge and belief are distinct yet intricately related components of an understanding of the way things are. Knowledge is "a complex operation of the examination of differences" limited by time and memory (Luhman, 1990, cited in Ahlemeyer, 2000, p. 3). Beliefs are understandings about the world based on evaluation and judgments thought to be true. They can be naive commonsense assumptions with little evidence of a theoretical knowledge base. Beliefs can also be informed and reflect an understanding of relevant concepts (Brownlee, Dart, Boulton-Lewis, and McCrindle, 1998).

Distinguishing knowledge from belief is difficult; beliefs are distinct from knowledge, although they underlie it. Belief systems are disputable, more inflexible, and less dynamic than knowledge systems, which are open to evaluation and critical examination. Beliefs filter new knowledge, discarding what conflicts and incorporating knowledge compatible with existing beliefs (Pajares, 1992). Belief change has a strong affective and emotional underpinning, as it involves cognitive conflict arising from mismatches between ideas and practices or dissatisfaction with existing notions (Ho, 2000). Challenges must produce sufficient discomfort to motivate a process of accommodation and change or rejection of beliefs that no longer fit with existing understandings. When no conflict is experienced, existing beliefs may be added to but not reconstructed.

The contemporary focus on knowledge as a social construction that produces and organizes differences invites learners to develop and change their ideas through the dissonant and disruptive effects of cognitive change. This position is supported by several versions of dissonance theory that maintain that the impetus for the construction of new knowledge stems from experience that provokes uncertainty (Festinger, 1957). This uncertainty has been variously described in the literature as an uncomfortable state (Tatum, 1992); disorientation and anxiety (Helms, 1995); disorientation (Mezirow, 1997); and the recognition of a discrepancy, conflict, or anomaly requiring resolution (Tillema, 1998). The conflict experienced between the realities of experience and existing preconceptions prompts change or resistance. Both the motivational needs of the perceiver, such as reaffirmation, and his or her attitudes toward members of a category identified as not normal have been found to hasten the process of stereotypic judgment and categorization (Hugenberg and Sacco, 2008). The next section considers the implications of this process and conceptual change.

Categorization and Conceptual Change

Categorization is the fundamental element of social cognition that shapes the way people perceive others. Categorical thinking is the process of assigning individuals to broad social categories according to their apparent similarities and differences. It also alerts the observer to any information that does not align with reasonable expectations of persons associated with a category (Macrae and Bodenhausen, 2000). Martha Minow (1990) highlights the dilemma of difference; whether it is attended to or ignored, social stigma results. She identifies the stereotyping and categorization of individuals as a process that cedes power to social definitions. In this way, notions of difference are embedded in categories as if they were inevitable and natural. As categorical notions are socially constructed, they may be challenged and changed through adult learning that promotes the examination of the assumptions embedded in social definitions and categories.

Currently, the indirect evidence of the mental models, concepts, and theories that people exhibit in actions and attitudes is the focus of research and study. Science education has been used as a medium to demonstrate what goes on in a learner's mind (Vosniadou, 2007). There is evidence that when new information conflicts with prior knowledge, learning processes promote a reorganization of the content of categories. This reorganization can change prior misconceptions and correct category mistakes (Chi, 2008; Minow, 1990). However, reorganization does not occur when prior ideas and practices are difficult to discard when the beliefs are deeply held. Instead, learners may select confirming evidence to resolve and dismiss cognitive conflict rather than engage in restructuring categories (Hashweh, 2003).

New approaches acknowledge that reconstruction of categories is accomplished in several ways. The first is a conceptual change approach that begins with existing perceptions and beliefs. Michelene Chi (2008) maintains that an ontological shift is required as, in her view, conceptual change involves the revision and restructure of the entire network of beliefs connecting concepts. A second approach considers commonsense notions that learners draw on to classify and guide their professional practice. These are more likely to be reformulated when explicitly challenged or invalidated either through direct experience or the processes of adult learning (Carbaroglu and Roberts, 2000). Hashweh (2003) investigated the way teachers use such cognitive reorganization to accommodate changes in knowledge, beliefs, and practice, including the role of dissonance in mediating inconsistencies and confusions. He noted the propensity of teachers to avoid conflict and search only for confirming evidence as a factor that hinders conceptual change.

Ableist Categorization and the Challenge for Adult Learners

Ableism is a relatively recent term. It implies "deeply held negative attitudes toward disability" (Hehir, 2005, p. 10) and shapes categories of "otherness" to which people are assigned on the basis of perceived difference. Central to ableism is the concept of norm or average because it simultaneously creates the idea of difference as abnormal deviance. These factors increase the likelihood that differences will be noticed and labeled in a more categorical way than may be the case when people are more critically aware of the controlling effect of hegemonic ideas of dis/ability. These ableist assumptions often play out in unconscious and unexamined ways on individual, institutional, and cultural levels. If adult educators really believe that disabled people should have ordinary lives, it is imperative that ways are found in training institutions such as higher and continuing education to draw attention to ableism and its effect on disabled people.

The literature of majority group identity development illustrates processes that can generate a greater consciousness of the injustice embedded in social systems and of individual attitudes and actions that maintain this situation. Models of the development of consciousness of white racial identity (Hardiman and Jackson, 1992; Helms 1995; Spanierman and Soble, 2010), heterosexual identity (Eliason, 1995), and the influence of ableism (McLean, 2005) all highlight the role of dissonance-inducing experiences in creating conditions that can promote conceptual change. Contact with people categorized as "other" produces difficult emotional reactions that are in conflict with acceptance of or apathy to their lived experience. Contact creates opportunities to challenge naiveté and initiate the development of an awareness of the impact of their own privileged status.

Role of Contact and Relationship

Without personal contact, nondisabled people remain unaffected by the presence of disability in the community. From the ableist position, the disabled state is "just there" (Linton, 1998). Institutions such as families, social networks, schools, and organizations facilitate contact. Social interaction is more likely to occur when disabled people live in the community and are encountered with high frequency as a consequence of friendship or employment. Other important factors include having time for contact, having an interest in disability, and not being afraid of people who are different.

Exposure to the experience of disablement starts with the opportunity to get to know a person with a disability through the development of relationships. Family relationships and friendships made through community and employment networks are common ways people become acquainted with the existence and impact of disability. Close family relationships, including a network of extended family members and the geographical proximity of families over a number of years, are factors that strengthen understandings of disability arising from kinship.

Friendship denotes the development and maintenance of close relationships through the exercise of social support, including the ability to ask friends to respond to or engage in an activity. Friendship also embraces the development of mutually interdependent relationships with disabled people. Such friendships may begin in childhood and include those formed at school with disabled classmates. Becoming aware of the experiences of families with children with physical or intellectual impairments can lead to a more sympathetic understanding of their difficulties. In these circumstances, friendship often involves a reciprocal process of social support, such as child-minding for short periods.

Some exposure to understandings that are in contention with ableist certainties and beliefs is also likely to occur in the course of a career that involves working with disabled adults and children. Getting to know someone with a disability can precipitate a move from indifference and ignorance to a better appreciation of the effects of disability. For contact to be a catalyst for the internal process of struggle, able-bodied people need to be capable of being affected by others' experience of disability. The quality of openness or sensitivity to the feelings and experience of others involves the recognition of features of mutuality and flexibility. This sensitivity promotes reflection and enables a changed response, including a reflective examination of the ways ableist actions might contribute to ongoing forms of oppression of disabled people.

Identities, including professional identities, derive from the relationships that are formed by contact with others (Fay, 1996). Professional relationships are often one-sided. While professionals may be quick to recognize disability or difference in others, it is more difficult for them to turn the gaze inward and recognize features of ableism within themselves or in a collective professional identity. Without contact with the experience of disability, the understandings and assumptions people may have about themselves and what they consider to be normal are likely to remain undisturbed. The process of coming to understand others leads to changes in both self-understanding and awareness of the effects of social interaction.

Challenging and Confronting Thinking

The movement from unconsciousness to consciousness, while internal to the individual, is provoked by the social context. Induced by the conflict of cognitive dissonance, this emotionally uncomfortable experience is referred to as "disintegration" for members of powerful groups and "dissonance" for members of marginalized groups (Festinger, 1957; Sleeter, 2001). The process of disintegration is characterized by internal struggles that arise from the need to find a resolution to incongruities and contradictions in beliefs and assumptions. Challenges to ableist naiveté about the real situation for disabled people can cause feelings of discomfort, including guilt, shame, and sometimes anger at the recognition of one's own advantage. Initially contact and social interaction are likely to cause some surprise that the

New Directions for Adult and Continuing Education • DOI: 10.1002/ace

societal stereotypes of people in marginalized groups do not match with the new experiences (Helms, 1990). One example is the realization that categorization as disabled is something nondisabled people do to others.

Another example is challenges to the established concept of normalcy, including its dubious use as an identifier of difference (Davis, 1997). Homogenizing forces that promote the acceptance of the prevailing norms lessen tolerance of difference. Normalcy is embedded in the beliefs, actions, and discourses that make up the fabric of everyday life. For the nondisabled person imbued with the tenets of normalcy, disability is a relative state characterized by a hierarchy of degrees of corporal misfortune. The effect of these notions is to privilege persons regarded as "able" while silencing and dominating those regarded as disabled.

Intense emotional experiences, such as those resulting from a sudden awareness of the effect of personal involvement in discriminatory social practice, provoke the disintegration of old meaning structures and the establishment of new ones. The affective dimension of learning also provides the substance for reflection that promotes the transformation of perspectives (Taylor, 2000). Sensitivity to the experience of others can facilitate an examination of unquestioned assumptions, in particular those related to the ableist view that disability is an inferior state based in biological impairment.

Practices in adult education assumed to be neutral and benevolent are also fields for challenge and critique. One effective practice is the employment of adult educators whose "private" identities as disabled or as parents of disabled children personify the challenges to ableist stereotypes. On one hand, such appointments assail ableist assumptions about competence as a marker of "normalcy." On the other, a sympathetic awareness can be fostered when students learn about the effects of ableist community views and begin to contrast the conditions in their own lives and with those prevailing for disabled people and their families.

Effect of Contact on Ableist Understandings of Disability

The development of a relationship with a disabled person can trigger a jolting or enlightening experience that impels movement away from hegemonic understandings. Such an experience can prompt the recognition of previously held ableist views. Significant personal distress, jarring events, crises, or disorienting dilemmas and integrating circumstances can trigger perspective transformation. Frank Rusch (2003, p. 63) writes of his eye-opening realization that "we and they are the same people." This was provoked when he began to understand the experience of behavior change procedures from the perspective of those subjected to them. Similar jolting realizations have been reported when adult learners become aware of the effects of ableism (McLean, 2008). The recognition of disability as a feature of ordinary human existence changes and challenges earlier conceptualizations of disability as personal tragedy and loss.

Personally experiencing the impact of social practices that marginalize others is another jolting experience. Getting out and about with people who use wheelchairs raises consciousness of the marginalizing effect of constructed environments. The acknowledgment of individual responsibility for the ableist response promotes an impetus for personal change. It is likely that both disabled and nondisabled persons will view the challenge of change with some wariness. As in the abandonment of racism, painful or insightful encounters can trigger the process of disestablishment (Helms, 1990). Participation makes possible the relationships with others that shape identity. The unearned advantages of being "able" are evoked in the context of adult education through the combination of study and its practical application. Since people had been struck by these insights, they were no longer able to remain oblivious to the effects of ableism on disabled people.

Changing beliefs is not possible without a challenge, as those beliefs form "an unknown protective wall against new information" (Tillema, 1998, p. 226). At any point on the journey toward developing a consciousness of ableism, the individual faces a choice either to remain oblivious to the situation or to move toward greater consciousness. The recognition of the personally advantageous position of not being disabled can increase consciousness of the ways in which ableism is maintained. At the same time, recognizing one's own advantage is an uncomfortable experience. To move from a position of indifference to one of concern about the social impact of disability requires sufficient flexibility to challenge, resist, or reconstruct established knowledge. Interaction with disabled people fosters empathy or openness to their experience.

Implications for Professional Development

If tertiary education is to implement the robust role assigned to it as a mediator in the current global context of economic, social, and cultural change (Organisation for Economic Co-operation and Development, 2003), then exposing the structures of inequality in society, including the ableist views perpetuated in learning and teaching about disability, is a legitimate task. A central research concern for adult educators remains this: how to overcome the influences of social power that limit the boundaries of understanding, especially in relation to the social effects of classifying perceived differences between groups of people (Gorman, 2000, cited in Clark, 2006). Our task is to support students through the discomforting discovery of structures of privilege and disadvantage inherent in institutionalized social positions. Maintaining a real commitment to social justice in adult education may involve the development of programs that purposefully foster relationships among diverse groups of people to increase the possibility of changing harmful preconceptions.

Service-learning is one model developed to integrate the objective of inclusive schooling into initial teacher education through a short period of experience in a range of voluntary support organizations in local communities (Carrington and Saggers, 2008). This model creates opportunities for relationships that promote the development of respect and empathy for people frequently regarded as different. The program employs reflection to assist students to examine their experience and develop a "more informed perspective about issues of marginalisation, segregation and injustice" (p. 803). Programs of study that occur alongside workplace experience therefore offer the opportunity for learners to become aware of their beliefs and their effects in practice.

Adult education can be an agent to change socially constructed views of disability. Opportunities to introduce nondisabled people to disabled people create the possibility they may get to know one another well. Where this occurs and there is provision to reflect on and challenge the conflicting ideas that arise from both interaction and a growing awareness of socially constructed conditions, there is the possibility of changing ableist beliefs. As John Ohliger observed: "When we impose ideas on people we train them. When we create an atmosphere in which people are free to explore ideas in dialogue and through interactions with other people, we educate them" (Ohliger, 1970, p. 250, cited in Wagner, 2009, p. 323).

With such principled direction, education may have a more sustained and transformative effect on understandings of normalcy, ability, and humanity that are required to protect the life chances of those most likely to be disregarded by the forces of late and globalized capitalism that shape contemporary social policy and practice.

References

Ahlemeyer, H. "Managing Organized Knowledge: A Systemic Proposal." *Journal of Sociocybernetics*, 2000, 2(1), 1–12. http://www.unizar.es/sociocybernetics/Journal/JoS1-2.pdf.

Brownlee, J., Dart, B., Boulton-Lewis, G., and McCrindle, A. "The Integration of Preservice Teachers' Naive and Informed Beliefs About Learning and Teaching." *Asia-Pacific Journal of Teacher Education*, 1998, 26(2), 107–120.

Carbaroglu, N., and Roberts, J. "Development in Student Teachers' Pre-existing Beliefs During a 1-Year PGCE Programme." *System*, 2000, 28, 387–402.

Carrington, S., and Saggers, B. "Service-Learning Informing the Development of an Inclusive Ethical Framework for Beginning Teachers." *Teaching and Teacher Education*, 2008, 24(3), 795–806.

Chi, M. "Three Types of Conceptual Change: Belief Revision, Mental Model Transformation and Categorical Shift." In S. Vosniadou (ed.), *International Handbook of Research on Conceptual Change*. New York: Routledge, 2008.

Clark, M. "Adult Education and Disability Studies, an Interdisciplinary Relationship: Research Implications for Adult Education." *Adult Education Quarterly*, 2006, 56(4), 308–322.

Davis, L. "Constructing Normalcy." In L. Davis (ed.), *The Disability Studies Reader*. New York: Routledge, 1997.

Eliason, M. "Accounts of Sexual Identity Formation in Heterosexual Students." *Sex Roles*, 1995, 32, 821–834.

Fay, B. *Contemporary Philosophy of Social Science: A Multicultural Approach*. Oxford, U.K.: Blackwell, 1996.

Festinger, L. A. *Theory of Cognitive Dissonance*. Stanford, Calif.: Stanford University Press, 1957.

Hardiman, R., and Jackson, B. "Racial Identity Development: Understanding Racial Dynamics in College Classrooms and on Campus." In M. Adams (ed.), *Promoting Diversity in College Classrooms*, no. 52. San Francisco: Jossey-Bass, 1992.

Hashweh, M. "Teacher Accommodative Change." *Teaching and Teacher Education*, 2003, 19(4), 421–434.

Hehir, T. *New Directions in Special Education*. Cambridge, Mass.: Harvard Education Press, 2005.

Helms, J. *Black and White Racial Identity: Theory, Research and Practice*. Westport, Conn: Greenwood Press, 1990.

Helms, J. "An Update of Helms' White and People of Color Racial Identity Models." In J. Ponterotto, J. Casas, L. Suzuki, and C. Alexander (eds.), *The Handbook of Multicultural Counseling*. Thousand Oaks, Calif.: Sage, 1995.

Ho, A. "A Conceptual Change Approach to Staff Development: A Model for Programme Design." *International Journal for Academic Development*, 2000, 5, 30–41.

Hugenberg, K., and Sacco, D. "Social Categorization and Stereotyping: How Social Categorization Biases Person Perception and Face Memory." *Social and Personality Psychology Compass*, 2008, 2(2), 1052–1072.

Komesaroff, L., and McLean, M. "Being There Is Not Enough: Inclusion Is Both Deaf and Hearing." *Deafness and Education International*, 2006, 8(2), 88–100.

Linton, S. *Claiming Disability: Knowledge and Identity*. New York: New York University Press, 1998.

Macrae, C. N., and Bodenhausen, G. "Social Cognition: Thinking Categorically About Others." *Annual Review of Psychology*, 2000, 51, 93–120.

McLean, M. "Emancipatory Understandings for Allies: Recognizing Ableism." In P. O'Brien and M. Sullivan (eds.), *Allies in Emancipation: Shifting from Providing Service to Being of Support*. Melbourne, Australia: Thomson Dunmore Press, 2005.

McLean, M. "Teaching About Disability: An Ethical Responsibility?" *International Journal of Inclusive Education*, 2008, 12(5–6), 605–619.

Mezirow, J. "Transformative Learning: Theory to Practice." In P. Cranton (ed.), *Transformative Learning in Action: Insights from Practice*. New Directions for Adult and Continuing Learning, no. 74. San Francisco: Jossey-Bass, 1997.

Minow, M. *Making All the Difference: Inclusion, Exclusion and American Law*. Ithaca, N.Y.: Cornell University Press, 1990.

Organisation for Economic Co-operation and Development. *Beyond Rhetoric: Adult Learning Policies and Practices*. Paris: Author, 2003.

Pajares, M. F. "Teachers' Beliefs and Educational Research: Cleaning Up a Messy Construct." *Review of Educational Research*, 1992, 62(3), 307–332.

Rusch, F. "Understanding Disabilities: The Emergence of Our Understanding of Sameness." In P. Devlieger, F. Rusch and D. Pfeiffer (eds.) *Rethinking Disability: The Emergence of New Definitions, Concepts and Communities*. Antwerp, Belgium: Garant, 2003.

Sleeter, C. *Culture, Difference and Power*. New York: Teachers College Press, 2001.

Spanierman, L., and Soble, J. "Understanding Whiteness." In J. Ponterotto, J. Manuel Casas, L. Suzuki, and C. Alexander (eds.), *Handbook of Multicultural Counseling*. Thousand Oaks, Calif.: Sage, 2010.

Tatum, B. "Talking About Race, Learning About Racism: The Application of Racial Identity Development Theory in the Classroom." *Harvard Educational Review*, 1992, *62*(1), 1–24.

Taylor, E. "Analyzing Research on Transformative Learning Theory." In J. Mezirow and Associates (eds.), *Learning as Transformation: Critical Perspectives on a Theory in Progress.* San Francisco: Jossey-Bass, 2000.

Tillema, H. "Stability and Change in Student Teachers' Beliefs About Teaching." *Teachers and Teaching: Theory and Practice*, 1998, *4*(2), 217–228.

Vosniadou, S. "Conceptual Change and Education." *Human Development*, 2007, *50*(1), 47–54.

Wagner, C. "John Ohliger's Legacy to Building Social Democracy WORTS and All." In A. P. Grace, T. S. Rocco, and M. R. Welton (eds.), *Challenging the Professionalization of Adult Education: John Ohliger and Contradictions in Modern Practice.* San Francisco: Jossey-Bass, 2009.

Ware, L. "A Moral Conversation on Disability: Risking the Personal in Educational Contexts." *Hypatia*, 2002, *17*(3), 143–172.

MARGARET A. MCLEAN is a senior lecturer in education studies (disability) at the University of Auckland. Her research interests are in the impact of ableism in tertiary-level education and curriculum design for professional development.

3

Medical and scientific research frequently has perpetuated the cycle of oppression by reinforcing the notion of disability as individual deviance rather than a sociopolitical issue.

Conducting Research with the Disability Community: A Rights-Based Approach

Kelly M. Munger, Donna M. Mertens

This chapter explores philosophical and theoretical frameworks that are useful for the conduct of research with people with disabilities. It then uses these frameworks as a basis for discussion of research practices, with a specific focus on differences that occur because of specific impairments and various cultural meanings of disability. The chapter provides examples of research with members of the disability community that illustrate culturally appropriate understandings of disability. These understandings can then be used as a basis for social change in the disability community to enhance the members' human rights.

Traditional Approaches to Research with the Disability Community

Approximately 54 million Americans, or one in every seven individuals, have a disability, making people with disabilities the largest minority group in the country. Yet this group also remains arguably the most oppressed minority group, as individuals with disabilities are far less likely to be employed, earn a college degree, and live independently as compared to their nondisabled counterparts (Charlton, 1998). Globally, nearly 85 percent of people with disabilities are impoverished, and in many areas of the world, educational and employment prospects for this group are virtually nonexistent (Charlton, 1998). This finding stems not from disabled individuals' innate functional limitations but from lack of opportunities to participate as equal and integral members of their communities.

NEW DIRECTIONS FOR ADULT AND CONTINUING EDUCATION, no. 132, Winter 2011 © 2011 Wiley Periodicals, Inc.
Published online in Wiley Online Library (wileyonlinelibrary.com) • DOI: 10.1002/ace.428

Medical and scientific research frequently has perpetuated the cycle of oppression by reinforcing the notion of disability as individual deviance rather than a sociopolitical issue. Much of this research has been highly medicalized, with doctors and other professionals assuming to know what disabled people want and need and frequently neglecting to ask disabled people their opinions at all. Indeed, throughout history, disabled individuals have been forced to serve as guinea pigs for medical experimentation that has no known or expected benefits for them. Although most people are familiar with the atrocities against disabled individuals in Nazi Germany, many remain unfamiliar with more recent programs, such as the Willowbrook study of the 1960s in Staten Island, New York, in which institutionalized children with intellectual disabilities were deliberately infected with hepatitis so that doctors could study the progression of the disease and could test new treatments (Riviera, 1972). In some parts of the world, these gross violations of human rights are still a regular occurrence.

Although these are extreme examples of research "on" disabled individuals, they are indicative of the general lack of respect that researchers traditionally have accorded this group. On a more positive note, research "for" individuals with disabilities has generally been designed with the goal of improving disabled people's lives by minimizing or ameliorating disease or impairment. Research generally is funded by impairment-specific organizations, such as the National Multiple Sclerosis Society or United Cerebral Palsy, whose general mission is to advance medical treatment for these conditions. In contrast to the examples described in the previous paragraph, the ultimate objective here is to genuinely help the individuals who experience these conditions; however, the research agendas generally are designed by nondisabled medical professionals who again frequently assume to know what people with disabilities want and need and also tend to see their population of interest (people with multiple sclerosis, people with cerebral palsy) as a single kind of person rather than as a diverse range of individuals with differing interests.

For example, while research for individuals with disabilities often has focused on medical treatments and cures, many disabled people themselves believe that they have a high quality of life even with their impairment and that their most serious difficulties stem not from their medical condition but from the way they remain socially oppressed and excluded from opportunities to participate in the mainstream. This is true even for individuals with very significant impairments, such as high-level spinal cord injuries (Albrecht and Devlieger, 1999; Gerhart, Koziol-McLain, Lowenstein, and Whiteneck, 1994; Mertens, Sullivan, and Stace, 2011).

Transformative Paradigm: An Overarching Umbrella for Disability Research

Given the historical legacy of discrimination against people with disabilities and the diversity within the disability community, an approach to research

New Directions for Adult and Continuing Education • DOI: 10.1002/ace

is needed that can provide an overarching umbrella that encompasses the complexity within these communities. The transformative paradigm offers such a framework. Guba and Lincoln's (2005) early work identified four philosophical assumptions that define a paradigm in social science research:

1. The *axiological* assumption, which refers to the nature of ethics
2. The *ontological* assumption, which refers to the nature of reality
3. The *epistemological* assumption, which refers to the nature of knowledge and the relationship between the researcher and the community of interest
4. The *methodological* assumption, which refers to the nature of systematic inquiry

The transformative paradigm (Mertens, 2009; 2010) is comprised of these four philosophical assumptions with priority placed on the pursuit of social justice and the furtherance of human rights. The transformative paradigm offers a metaphysical umbrella that brings together commensurate philosophical strands. It is applicable to people who experience discrimination and oppression on whatever basis, including (but not limited to) race/ethnicity, disability, immigrant status, political conflicts, sexual orientation, poverty, gender, age, or the multitude of other characteristics that are associated with less access to social justice. In addition, the transformative paradigm is applicable to the study of the power structures that perpetuate social inequities (Mertens, 2009).

The philosophical assumptions associated with the transformative paradigm provide a framework for exploring the use of a social justice lens in research. An examination of the status of human rights protections and violations is needed to explicitly address the goal of promoting social justice and furthering human rights. The transformative paradigm is based on recognition of human rights as they are articulated by the United Nations (UN) and as they are understood in the targeted communities. The UN (1948) passed a universal declaration of human rights in the 1940s. It would seem that a universal declaration would mean that the rights of people from all walks of life would be protected. However, the UN acknowledges that specific groups of people have not had their rights protected and enforced; therefore, the organization undertook to recognize those constituencies by passing resolutions that recognize the rights of women (1979), racial minorities (1969), children (1990a), migrant workers (1990b), people with disabilities (2006a), and indigenous peoples (2006b). This is a partial listing of subgroups whose rights need to be consciously addressed in research that is conducted with an awareness of the diversity within the disability communities. Dimensions of diversity are contextually dependent; different dimensions will be of relevance in different research.

New Directions for Adult and Continuing Education • DOI: 10.1002/ace

Transformative Axiological Assumption. The axiological belief is the first-listed of the transformative assumptions because it has a critical influence on the character of the subsequent assumptions. Researchers might ask themselves such questions as: What are the ethical principles that guide my work? What is the connection between those ethical principles and issues of social justice? How do the ethical principles reflect issues of culture and power differences? How can this research contribute to social justice and human rights? If I accept that this is a desirable goal for research, what would I do differently in terms of methodology?

To conduct an ethical transformative research study, researchers need to be able to identify the cultural norms and beliefs that are present in the communities in which we work. If we are to act respectfully, then we need to include mechanisms for entering communities that permit the identification of these cultural norms and beliefs and to understand the implications of those norms to support either the pursuit of human rights or those that are used to sustain an oppressive system. Such an ethical assumption calls on us to be proactive in the identification of cultural beliefs and norms and to be interactive with community members to solicit their understandings of how those norms and beliefs impact their lives. In order to be inclusive of a variety of beliefs and norms, researchers need also to be aware of relevant cultural groups in the context of the inquiry and the cultural norms associated with those groups.

As researchers, it is easy to focus only on problems in a community. However, such a focus ignores the strengths and resilience in communities. Rather than painting a picture of a downtrodden, victimized community, researchers should be aware of the strengths in communities and make sure that those are brought to light along with the challenges that community members experience. In addition, researchers should be cognizant of the history of researchers taking information from communities without giving anything in return. There is a need to consider how the research findings can be used to sustain change in the community when the researchers leave or how to give proactive attention to issues of sustainability. At the same time, researchers have an ethical obligation to clearly communicate the limitations of their work in terms of being realistic about the potential for changes.

The transformative methodological assumption is discussed later in this chapter. However, each of the transformative assumptions has implications for methodological decisions and criteria for determining if the assumptions have been realized. For example, the transformative axiological assumption suggests that researchers ask questions to critically examine the consistency of their ethical beliefs and their methods choices, such as:

- To what extent is the researcher able to identify cultural norms and beliefs within communities that are supportive of or deleterious to the pursuit of social justice and human rights?

- How do researchers demonstrate that they have taken action to support those norms and beliefs that support human rights and social justice and challenge those that sustain an oppressive system?
- How do researchers demonstrate that they are leaving the community better off than when they began the research in terms of increased knowledge, capacity, or changes in policies or practices?
- In what ways was the research framed to take into account the expertise, knowledge, and strengths of the community in order to provide a platform for authentic engagement between the researcher and the community?
- How does the research address the sustainability of the changes in the community that provide for the possibility of taking action to enhance social justice and human rights after the researcher leaves the community?

Transformative Ontological Assumption. The logical connection between the axiological and ontological assumptions is clear. If some cultural norms and beliefs support the enhancement of social justice and human rights and some do not, the researcher needs to design the research so that it can reveal those different versions of reality and to understand the dimensions of diversity that influence which versions of reality are given privilege. The researcher also needs to build in mechanisms to reveal versions of reality that sustain oppressive systems and those that have the potential to further human rights. These beliefs and their implications for methodological decisions lead to criteria to assess the quality of research studies that include:

- To what extent did the researcher reveal different versions of reality?
- How did the researcher determine those versions of reality that have the potential to either support or impede progress toward social justice and human rights?
- What were the consequences of identifying these versions of reality?
- How did this research contribute to the change in understandings of what is real?

Transformative Epistemological Assumption. The transformative epistemological assumption explores the nature of knowledge and the relationship between the knower and that which would be known, or, in research parlance, between the researcher and the stakeholders. In order for researchers to design and implement research studies that are commensurate with the assumptions that have been explained previously, they need to establish an interactive link between themselves and the full range of stakeholders. Taking the word of the most powerful about the viewpoints of the least powerful can result in research that does not address the most important concerns of the least powerful. Thus, criteria for quality in methods related to the transformative epistemological assumption include:

- What is the nature of the relationship between the researcher and the stakeholders?
- What evidence is there that the researcher explicitly addressed issues of power differentials and that the voices of the least powerful are accurately expressed and acted on?
- How did the researcher establish a trusting relationship with the stakeholders?

Researchers need to understand appropriate strategies for entering cultural groups in order to establish relationships that have the potential to contribute to social transformation. When researchers attempt to enter cultural groups that are not reflective of their own backgrounds, they need to investigate and make use of appropriate strategies for entry by reading and consulting with members of the community. For example, when Mertens entered the deaf community as a hearing professor at Gallaudet University, she had to learn American Sign Language and Deaf culture. After 30 years in that environment, she is comfortable communicating and interacting with members of the Deaf community who use American Sign Language. However, she still describes herself as a learner because American Sign Language is not her native language and the Deaf community is not her home culture. She also knows that the American Sign Language Deaf group represents only one portion of the deaf population. In order to interact respectfully with other people who are deaf, she needs to consult with members of these other deaf subgroups. For example, if deaf people lip read and use assistive listening devices, it is very important to face them and to speak distinctively to provide appropriate information needed for communication.

Researchers who are not working in their native language or in their home culture may not have 30 years to establish their credibility in communities. Therefore, they might need to use other strategies. Importantly, researchers need to present themselves and their backgrounds in ways that make clear their strengths and limitations in terms of their knowledge and life experiences. This positioning allows researchers to acknowledge the need to work together with people from the community who have a stronger understanding of cultural and social issues.

Other strategies that are useful in this context include establishing research teams that are reflective of members of the community and forming relationships with important community gatekeepers who can stand beside the researchers and vouch for their credibility. For example, Mertens, Holmes, Harris, and Brandt (2007) formed a team to evaluate a federally funded teacher preparation program. The program was designed to recruit and support teachers who were deaf or hard of hearing in order to increase the number of teachers who reflect the same characteristics as deaf students. Hearing applicants were also accepted into the program. The program was focused on the preparation of teachers to teach deaf students who have an additional disability.[1] They developed the team with one hearing researcher, two culturally Deaf native users of American Sign Language, and one deaf researcher who uses a cochlear implant and knows American Sign Language but is not a native user. Thus, they were able to represent the variety of cultural groups that were taking part in the program. This allowed them to match the communication preferences of the participants during the collection of data. Deaf American Sign Language users were interviewed by the two Deaf American Sign Language researchers working together. The hearing participants were interviewed by the hearing researcher and the researcher who used a cochlear implant working together.

Transformative Methodological Assumption. The transformative methodological assumption does not mandate the use of any particular method. However, it does provide the rationale for choosing to use mixed methods in order to be consistent with the other transformative assumptions within the context of community responsiveness. Researchers need qualitative/dialogic moments in the beginning of their planning to ascertain the cultural context in which they are working. The use of qualitative and quantitative data facilitates responsiveness to different stakeholders and issues. Mixed methods can also be used to capture the contextual complexity and provide pluralistic avenues for appropriately engaging with diverse cultural groups in the research. To this end, criteria for quality related to the transformative methodological assumption include:

- How was a cyclical design used to make use of interim findings throughout the study?
- To what extent did researchers engage with the full range of stakeholders to gather qualitative data that enhance their understandings of the community?
- How were data collection methods used in order to be responsive to the needs of diverse stakeholders?
- To what extent were the methods used responsive to the specific needs of the different stakeholder groups?
- How were the methodologies designed to enhance use of the research findings to support the pursuit of social justice and human rights?

Example of the Transformative Research Paradigm

An extended illustration from Munger's (2011) research with individuals with cerebral palsy (CP) shows how each of the transformative assumptions can be utilized in practice. In her research, Munger wanted to develop an understanding of how adults with CP experience their social and psychological worlds. As CP is a developmental disability, the research on individuals with CP has focused almost exclusively on children. The little research that focuses on adults has been conducted primarily from a very positivist and deficit-based perspective. In contrast, Munger, who herself has CP, utilized a strengths-based approach in her qualitative research, eliciting personal narratives from research informants with CP concerning how they derive meaning from their personal relationships and everyday interactions with others.

Utilizing multiple data collection strategies, including two extended interviews, a diary study, and an online focus group, Munger sought to capture study participants' genuine lived experience, particularly as related to their sense of social devaluation. Munger believed that those with CP would be particularly prone to experience stigma and social oppression because of their often-unique form of embodiment, difficulties controlling their bodies and bodily functions, communication differences, and others' assumptions that their physical challenges automatically implied diminished intellectual abilities. Discussions with participants confirmed this belief. Consistent with the transformative axiological assumption, many participants described how widespread cultural beliefs about disability in general and CP in particular resulted in others' patronizing behavior. One participant told a story of a stranger who called the police after he stopped her on the street to ask for directions to a party; another described an incident in which a hotel clerk refused to accept his credit card, believing that it had been stolen. Participants explained with eloquence how it was not their impairment that interfered with their overall well-being but the ways in which they were treated by others.

In fact, most participants demonstrated great resilience, indicating that they were quite satisfied with who they were and would not accept a cure for their CP if offered one. Contrary to popular opinion about how difficult and unfortunate it must be to use a wheelchair or to require a computerized device to communicate, even the most functionally limited participant in the group described having CP as "awesome." Consistent with the transformative ontological assumption, these examples illustrate the importance of research designs that encourage participants to convey their own personal realities, particularly when those realities exemplify the value of human diversity and social justice.

Throughout the entire research process, Munger had to remain very cognizant of her own position as a researcher. Consistent with the transformative epistemological assumption, Munger sought to establish her participants' trust by creating a warm, welcoming environment in which to relate their stories. However, while the common experience of CP was helpful in establishing credibility and facilitating openness, it also proved to be challenging in certain instances when participants felt that she intuitively understood their experiences and so there was no need to describe them in detail. Encouraging participants to acknowledge the complexity and value of their unique experience as individuals rather than as "just another person with cerebral palsy" was instrumental in overcoming this challenge. Moreover, although Munger's own position certainly contributed to her interpretations of participants' experiences (it was impossible to divorce herself from CP), she remained mindful of how it might cloud her judgment and worked to counteract any biases (e.g., by comparing her analyses with those of outside reviewers).

Consistent with the transformative methodological assumption, Munger worked to design her investigation to accommodate the needs of her participants and to allow them to fully express themselves. For instance, while all individuals participated in all phases of data collection, participants with communication challenges were often able to provide richer data through their written diaries than through the individual interviews. In contrast, those with difficulty typing were offered the opportunity to dictate their focus group responses to Munger, who then posted them to the focus group discussion board. By finding creative solutions to facilitate everyone's involvement, not only was Munger able collect more valuable data, but she also created a supportive peer-to-peer community. Finally, through pilot testing her interview guides and asking participants and outside auditors with CP to provide feedback on her major findings, Munger worked to involve constituents from the study population in multiple stages of the research project.

The examples described in this chapter are based on research with deaf people and people with CP. Readers interested in transformative research with other disability groups can access information through the organizations listed in Table 3.1. The table provides several Web sites containing a diverse array of examples of disability-related research and activities that work to promote social justice.

Conclusion

This chapter addresses the importance of conducting research with the disability community in ways that promote social justice and provide disabled individuals with expanded opportunities. By adhering to the assumptions underlying the transformative paradigm, researchers can gain a fuller understanding of the genuine lived experiences of people with disabilities while simultaneously and steadfastly working to better those experiences. Challenges remain, but the transformative paradigm provides one pathway by which research with people with disabilities can support social change in the name of social justice.

Table 3.1 Organizations Conducting Research Pertaining to Disability and Social Justice

Organization	Description and Web Site
Disabled Persons International	Network of national organizations to promote the human rights of disabled people through full participation, equalization of opportunity, and development www.dpi.org
Social Justice Research Centre, Edith Cowan University	Researches a wide range of issues related to disability and social justice www.psychology.ecu.edu.au/research/social-justice/disabilities.php
Center for Capacity Building for Minorities with Disabilities Research	Conducts participatory action research with community members and agencies; documents impact of social services www.uic.edu/orgs/empower/Center%20web%20page/ccbmdr.htm
Disability Rights Education and Defense Fund	Works to advance the civil and human rights of people with disabilities through legal advocacy, training, education, and public policy and legislative development www.dredf.org/about/index.shtml
Center on Human Policy, Law, and Disability Studies	Conducts research to promote the rights of people with disabilities and the idea of disability as an integral aspect of diversity in society http://disabilitystudies.syr.edu

Note

1. Members of the Deaf community view themselves as a cultural group who have their own languages, values, and shared behavior patterns. They do not view themselves as having a disability. Therefore, if a person who is Deaf has a disability such as blindness or cerebral palsy, they describe themselves as Deaf with a disability.

References

Albrecht, G. L., and Devlieger, P. J. "The Disability Paradox: High Quality of Life Against All Odds." *Social Science and Medicine*, 1999, *48*, 977–988.

Charlton, J. I. *Nothing About Us Without Us: Disability Oppression and Empowerment.* Berkeley: University of California Press, 1998.

Gerhart, K. A., Koziol-McLain, J., Lowenstein, S. R., and Whiteneck, G. G. "Quality of Life Following Spinal Cord Injury: Knowledge and Attitudes of Emergency Care Providers." *Annals of Emergency Medicine*, 1994, *23*(4), 807–812.

Guba, E. G., and Lincoln, Y. S. (eds.) *Handbook of Qualitative Research*. Thousand Oaks, Calif.: Sage, 2005.

Mertens, D. M. *Research and Evaluation in Education and Psychology: Integrating Diversity with Quantitative, Qualitative, and Mixed Methods*, 3rd ed. Thousand Oaks, Calif.: Sage, 2010.

Mertens, D. M. *Transformative Research and Evaluation*. New York: Guilford Press, 2009.

Mertens, D. M., Holmes, H., Harris, H., and Brandt, S. *Project SUCCESS: Summative Evaluation Report*. Washington, D.C.: Gallaudet, 2007.

Mertens, D. M., Sullivan, M., and Stace, H. "Disability Communities: Transformative Research and Social Justice." In N. K. Denzin and Y. S. Lincoln (eds.), *Handbook of Qualitative Research*, 4th ed. Thousand Oaks, Calif.: Sage, 2011.

Munger, K. "Telling a Different Story: Marginality and Resilience in the Everyday Lives of Adults with Cerebral Palsy." Unpublished doctoral dissertation, University of Illinois-Chicago, 2011

Rivera, G. *Willowbrook: A Report on How It Is and Why It Doesn't Have to Be That Way*. New York: Random House, 1972.

United Nations. Universal Declaration of Human Rights. 1948. www.un.org/Overview/rights.html.

United Nations. The International Convention on the Elimination of All Forms of Racial Discrimination. New York: Author, 1969. www2.ohchr.org/english/law/cerd.htm.

United Nations. The Convention on the Elimination of All Forms of Discrimination Against Women (CEDAW). New York: Author, 1979. www.un.org/womenwatch/daw/cedaw/text/econvention.htm.

United Nations. Convention on the Rights of the Child. New York: Author, 1990a. www2.ohchr.org/english/law/crc.htm.

United Nations. International Convention on the Protection of the Rights of All Migrant Workers and Members of Their Families. New York: Author, 1990b. www.un.org/millennium/law/iv-13.htm.

United Nations. Convention on the Rights of People with Disabilities. New York: Author, 2006a. www.un.org/disabilities/convention/conventionfull.shtml.

United Nations. Declaration of Rights of Indigenous Peoples. Adopted by the General Assembly 13 September 2007. New York: Author, 2006b. www.un.org/esa/socdev/unpfii/en/declaration.html.

KELLY M. MUNGER *is a Ph.D. candidate in disability studies at the University of Illinois-Chicago. With a specific interest in adults with cerebral palsy, she focuses on the psychology of disability and everyday experiences of devaluation and resilience.*

DONNA M. MERTENS *is a professor at Gallaudet University, where she teaches research design and program research to deaf students. She focuses on issues related to social justice and human rights for people with disabilities through research approaches.*

4

The American Psychiatric Association estimates that over 17 million Americans currently suffer from severe clinical depression. Learning how to live with and fight such depression must therefore be considered a massive societal adult learning task.

When the Black Dog Barks: An Autoethnography of Adult Learning in and on Clinical Depression

Stephen Brookfield

The U.S. government's National Institute of Mental Health (NIMH) estimates that in any given year, 14.8 million American adults (about 6.7 percent of the adult population) suffer from clinical depression or major depressive disorder, as it is sometimes called (NIMH, n.d.). In Canada, a recent study projected the estimate of sufferers much higher than had previously been imagined, calculating that 19.7 percent of adults suffer from clinical depression sometime during their lifetime (Boughton, 2009). The NIMH also classifies clinical depression as the leading form of disability for Americans ages 15 to 44. Depression is not feeling sad at the loss of a loved one; it is not being devastated by a marriage breakup or feeling a loss of identity after being fired. Neither is it feeling trapped by winter in northern climes with the resultant lack of natural light or sun. All these things are traumatic and distressing, but all are traceable to a specific root cause. In this chapter, I am defining depression as the persistent feeling of complete worthlessness and hopelessness, often accompanied by the overwhelming anxiety that this hour, this day, or this week will be your last on earth. This kind of depression has no clearly identifiable social cause, such as death, divorce, or economic crisis; instead, it settles on you uninvited, and often completely unexpected, and permeates your soul, flesh, and bone.

Winston Churchill described his own depression as the black dog that prowled constantly on the edge of his consciousness. He never knew when the black dog would appear, but it became an almost constant companion— just as the presence of a dog that is a family pet is woven into the fabric of

New Directions for Adult and Continuing Education, no. 132, Winter 2011 © 2011 Wiley Periodicals, Inc.
Published online in Wiley Online Library (wileyonlinelibrary.com) • DOI: 10.1002/ace.429

your daily life. Clinical depression is like that—quotidian, everyday, the first thing you're aware of as you open your eyes and the last thing you think about as you drift off to sleep (if you're lucky enough to be able to sleep). Its very familiarity, its relentless presence, is itself terrifying, suggesting that it will always dog you (pun intended). As someone who suffers from depression and who has spent over a decade experimenting with how to function with this condition as part of my everyday life, I can speak with experiential authority about this topic.

Everyone reading these words has probably either suffered from depression or knows someone who has. Yet the stigma surrounding mental illness means that it is rare to hear people admit to this. It is easier to hide and disguise depression than it is to hide physical disability or other severe mental disorders, such as schizophrenia. You can pretend to be overworked, needing more sleep, stressed, fed up, worried about your job, having difficulties in your relationship, or lonely—and people will see these as part of the ups and downs of everyday life. In my own case, I spent many years hiding depression from every human being I interacted with (including my children) other than my wife and my brothers. In this chapter, I wish to use my own experience of learning to understand and cope with depression as the starting point for an analysis of what might comprise a research agenda for anyone interested in exploring the adult learning dimensions of depression. The numbers quoted at the start of this chapter indicate that learning how to live with, and treat, depression must be considered a massive societal adult learning task. Such a task comprises two dimensions: requiring (1) adults to learn how to recognize, monitor, and cope with such depression and (2) adult educators to provide education about this condition. I intend to explore the first of these dimensions: how adults learn to deal with the onset of depression. In doing so, I marry some prevailing paradigms in adult education to an autoethnography of clinical depression.

I am a well-published author in the field of adult education who has a fulfilling job, a loving family, and a rich avocational life focusing on soccer and music. Objectively I have absolutely nothing to be depressed about. True, I have suffered predictable life crises—the death of parents, divorce, being fired, and various health problems—but by most people's estimate I live a life of enormous privilege. For over a decade, however, I have suffered from crippling clinical depression that has overshadowed everything that I do. This depression has caused me periodically to remove myself from professional engagements (usually pleading a physical health crisis or other conflicting professional engagement as the cause) and, at its worst, has confined me to home. Many days I do not know how I will make it through the next fifteen minutes without knocking myself out to ensure oblivion. At its worst, I spend the day longing for evening when I can take a sleeping pill and get the five hours of oblivion it ensures. My barometer for measuring each day has changed dramatically from "What did I accomplish today?" to

New Directions for Adult and Continuing Education • DOI: 10.1002/ace

"Did I feel suicidal for most of the day?" A day when I don't feel suicidal these days is a gift from God, a day to treasure.

Learning Tasks of Depression

Drawing on my own autoethnography, I posit that four distinctive learning tasks are required in seeking to live with depression. The first three of these have little to do with technical learning or with understanding pharmaceutical or psychotherapeutic treatment options. Instead, they are concerned with changes in perspective, with developing emotional intelligence, with ideological detoxification.

Overcoming Shame. The first, and perhaps most fundamental, task is learning to live with the shame that depression induces. The feelings of worthlessness and inadequacy that accompany not being able to do the simplest daily things that were so unremarkable in the past are debilitating, sending you spiraling down farther and farther into the vortex of depression. As you tell yourself for the hundredth time that day to snap out of it—and are unable to do so—it is easy to be enveloped in self-disgust. You feel weak and helpless. It's so clear, you tell yourself, that there's no objective reason to be depressed. But saying this only makes the situation worse. After all, if there's no reason to be depressed, then your inability to escape this state means you have no willpower, no determination, no initiative.

Getting these feelings of weakness and shame under control were extraordinarily difficult for me. But two adult educational concepts helped me here. The first was to try to apply the critical reflection I had urged on others in writings and workshops to my own situation. I realized over time that I was trapped in two paradigmatic assumptions. A paradigmatic assumption is a framing, structuring assumption that we hold. It is so close to us, so much a part of who we are and how we view the world, that when someone points it out to us, we usually deny that it's an assumption and instead claim, "That's the way the world is." Moreover, when we do start to identify and assess paradigmatic assumptions, the effect is often explosive, changing completely how we look at, and respond to, a situation. It seems to me that challenging a paradigmatic assumption warrants consideration as an example of the much-invoked concept of transformative learning (Cranton and Taylor, forthcoming).

The first paradigmatic assumption I had to uncover had to do with the etiology of depression. I assumed that people feel depressed because something bad has happened to them. So the fact that depression had settled on me seemingly out of the blue was completely puzzling. Yes, 9/11 had happened a few months before, and, yes, I had nursed my mother during her last weeks of cancer a year earlier, and, yes, some test results had been worrying—but none of those seemed to account for the overwhelming anxiety and depression that gripped me. The paradigmatic assumption that depression was rationally caused, and therefore treated by the application of reason, took me years to unearth, challenge, and discard. I had always considered myself a sentimental person, given to emotional reactions to people, compassion, sport, music, and film, and had no idea of just how deeply the epistemology of European rationality was assimilated within me. Challenging and changing this assumption with the assumption that depression was the result of chemical imbalances in the brain was enormously difficult. I was so fixated on my inability to reason myself out of feeling depressed that I was unable to consider any other way of understanding how depression was caused.

A major stumbling block in switching my meaning schemes here was the lack of public conversation about depression. Nobody I knew at work had mentioned being treated for depression, there was nothing I remember reading about it in the press or seeing on TV, and I couldn't think of a single film that dealt with it, other than *About a Boy*, where a mother's depression is a minor plot thread. One result of my understanding how little public conversation there was on learning how to live with depression was that I resolved once I began to feel more stable that I would speak publicly about my own experiences whenever possible. One must learn disclosure. One must learn to talk about this condition to one's partner, spouse, friends, parents, siblings, in-laws, children, and colleagues. Somehow, in almost every speech and workshop I give these days, I try to weave in some examples of my own struggles with depression. One of the benefits of public disclosure is finding just how many others suffer from the same disease. Invariably, when I talk about learning around depression, I have several people come up to me at the end of the session and tell me how much they appreciated it.

Having managed to reframe my assumptions about the etiology of depression, it became much easier to keep the debilitating effects of shame under control. If depression is linked to chemical imbalances in the brain, I could tell myself, then part of its treatment has to be pharmaceutical. Suddenly, drugs didn't seem a sign of weakness, an indication that I was a pathetic excuse as a human being. After all, my psychiatrist told me, you're fine with taking drugs for bodily imbalances such as high cholesterol, high blood pressure, acid reflux—why should taking drugs to redress chemical imbalances be any different?

Ideological Detoxification. But a second paradigmatic assumption, just as deeply embedded as my assumption that depression was rationally caused and therefore treated with reason, was also in play. This assumption was that patriarchy—the ideology that holds men to be superior reasoning beings, ruled by logic in decision making (as against women, who are held to be victims of irrationality, ruled only by emotion)—was a legitimate view of the world. Now if you had asked me what I thought of patriarchy, I would have told you it was a destructive ideology, one I rejected unequivocally. But I have learned that what I think are my obvious, conscious, commitments often mask much a deeper and more enduring acceptance of dominant ideology.

New Directions for Adult and Continuing Education • DOI: 10.1002/ace

I am convinced that one reason I could not shake my feeling of shame was of my uncritical acceptance of the ideology of patriarchy. "I'm a man, I'm supposed to be ruled by reason, I should be able to keep my feelings under control" was the inner voice that rumbled beneath my more conscious conversations. To take drugs to deal with a problem was something that would be OK if I was a woman but was surely a sign of weakness for a man. So month after month, year after year, I refused to consider any suggestion of medication. This refusal was underscored by the fact that the only people I knew who were taking medication for mental problems were women. There was no male I was aware of taking medication for depression.

One thing I learned about overcoming shame was that for me, a man, it required a process of ideological detoxification. I had to understand just how deeply and powerfully the ideology of patriarchy had been implanted in me over my five decades on the planet. And I had to understand too that stopping it from determining how I thought about, and responded to, my own depression would be a long haul. Even today, despite having written books on critical theory (Brookfield, 2004) and radicalizing learning (Brookfield and Holst, 2010)—both of which explore how to resist ideological manipulation—I still feel there's an unseemly lack of manliness, or grit, in my suffering from and disclosing about my depression.

Normalizing Despair. A third task is to learn how to normalize depression, to view it as something that is as unremarkable as possible. When you suffer from depression, it's easy to conclude that you're the only one in this situation. The more isolated you feel, the more you believe that your situation is unique, that there are no supports in place for you, and that there is nobody else who experiences what you experience. The sort of public disclosure I wrote about in the previous section is one way counter to this. But there is another, more private, learning process to undertake that also helps to manage depression: learning how to do a realistic audit of what it is reasonable to hope for in the face of numbing dread and vulnerability.

One thing sufferers of depression learn is to take one day at a time. Instead of gauging your ability to function by whether you are depression free or not, you learn to calibrate hour-by-hour changes. Progress is measured by how many minutes you focus on a task with your thoughts only on that task, or by whether your attention was distracted for periods in a sporting or musical event. When you're mired in depression, the prospect of coming out of it seems so unreachable, so improbable, that judging your progress by how close you come to that state only sends you into deeper depression. You learn to adjust what is reasonable to expect to fit what is possible. For example, when I am depressed, I define a great day as being one where I am not feeling suicidal.

Learning to normalize despair is, like so much of learning how to live with depression, something that involves different processes. You have to engage in social learning (learning how to use peers and fellow sufferers for emotional support and information) if you are to realize that what seems like your unique misery has generic elements embedded within it. Learning to overcome shame and move to self-disclosure is, as we have already seen, a major hurdle. Normalizing learning also entails maintaining hope in the face of adversity, hanging on to the belief that sometime in the future you will feel better than you do today. Such hope is like a candle flickering in the hurricane winds of dread and anxiety that sweep over you.

Calibrating Treatment. The study of brain chemistry is still in its infancy. One medical professional knowledgeable in this area told me that in 50 years, the standard approaches we use to treat depression will appear laughably ill informed. But one thing that is clear is that each person's chemistry is different and that each person's case therefore requires considerable research and individual experimentation. The major part of the responsibility for this research obviously rests with the prescribing physician, whether psychiatrist or family practitioner, and also with any psychologist or therapist involved. However, the patient suffering from depression also has a role to play in monitoring how drugs or talk therapy work; the conditions under which they are most, or least, effective; what the different portions of each should be; whether the side effects (often unpleasant) of drugs are worth the distraction or relief they provide; and on and on.

The only reason I can write this chapter is that after several years of debilitating psychological torture, I finally found a cocktail of drugs that keeps me intact. Doing this involved a lot of technical, trial-and-error sorts of learning. I had to learn how to calibrate the right mix of medication, cognitive behavioral therapy, exercise, meditation, avoidance, and homeopathic remedies to find the combination that was uniquely suited to reducing my depression. I know my depression will not disappear, but through persistence and luck, it is (at least, for the moment) kept at a level that is not wholly debilitating.

I have already written about some of the crucial decisions in my learning how to calibrate treatment—my decision to overcome my shame, detoxify myself from patriarchy, and normalize my despair. But, once I made the decision to seek professional help, I then had to decide what kind of help was going to be most effective. I saw three family practitioners, four psychologists, and two psychiatrists in my quest to learn which combination of approaches would work for me. A major stumbling block for me was my unwillingness to change psychiatrists. I was working with a psychiatrist whose approach was one I agreed with philosophically. He believed the ultimate responsibility for treatment decisions lay squarely with the patient. So when experiencing the unpleasant side effects of antidepressants, I repeatedly would come off medications after a short period. My treating psychiatrist would respond by saying that since one treatment option wasn't working, we would move to another.

My wife would often tell me that I needed a psychiatrist who would be more proactive and unequivocal about the need for me to stay on a course of medication for more than a few weeks. I would dismiss her opinion as that of an unqualified professional, not realizing that the person who knew me best was in many ways the best person to judge what kind of psychiatric approach would be of most benefit to me. Eventually, I became so distraught that in desperation I followed her advice and managed to get an appointment with a different psychiatrist. This professional insisted I needed to get on a long-term course of medication immediately and gave me a short-term prescription of a powerful antianxiety drug that would help control the worst side effects of the long-term medication. As soon as we left the consulting room, my wife told me he was by far a more suitable person to be overseeing my treatment and that his directive approach was exactly what I needed.

Conclusion

What are the implications of my autoethnography for how adult education might engage itself with the study of depression? Several items suggest themselves to me. First, we need a greater elaboration of the learning tasks I outlined, plus all the other learning tasks entailed by learning to recognize and cope with depression. To use Habermas's (1979) often-quoted formulation, some of these learning tasks will be instrumental (such as calibrating doses and combinations of medicine, practicing cognitive behavioral therapy). Some will be communicative, such as learning how to interpret medical advice from experts or how to communicate one's situation to colleagues, peers, and family members. Some will surely be emancipatory, such as challenging dominant ideology's stigmatization of medical illness. Probably, most of the learning tasks people identify will cross all three domains; after all, learning to manage medication levels leads to a liberatory feeling of self-confidence and a willingness to go public about one's own depression.

Second, the methods of learning most frequently associated with each task can be studied. Which of these involve mostly self-directed learning? Which entail learning from an authoritative teacher, such as a therapist or psychiatrist? Which learning tasks are social in nature, distinguished by the learner's immersion in a social network? What is the progression of methodologies? What methods most support a willingness to challenge dominant ideology? Are certain kinds of learning tasks best accomplished through particular methods, or is the personality type of the learner more important? What role do cultural factors play in disclosing and seeking treatment for depression?

Third, some of the field's prevailing theoretical paradigms can be applied to understanding depression. Coping successfully with depression is certainly an example of transformative learning, and it requires an enormous amount of critical reflection. Therapists, psychiatrists, and other physicians act as adult educators concerned to empower patients to monitor and treat their own depression in a self-directed manner. From a critical theory perspective, one might ask: What does the stratification of depression look like? Are some groups more prone to depression, or does it escape easy location? How does the political economy of healthcare determine who has access to treatment? And how does professional power label some treatment options as legitimate and some as irresponsible? From a feminist perspective, one might explore how women create support groups to connect their struggles to a broader network or the degree to which learning to disclose depression is a function of gender identity. From a racialized perspective, one might analyze an Africentric approach to depression, in which individual consciousness is understood always to be located in community, or a Confucian approach, in which reverence for expert wisdom is the preferred approach for solving problems. In sum, clinical depression represents a major area for adult education research.

References

Boughton, B. "Lifetime Prevalence of Depression Twice as High as Previous Estimates." *Medscape Today*, 2009 (June). www.medscape.com/viewarticle/703754.

Brookfield, S. D. *The Power of Critical Theory: Liberating Adult Learning and Teaching.* San Francisco: Jossey-Bass, 2004.

Brookfield, S. D., and Holst, J. D. *Radicalizing Learning: Adult Education for a Just World.* San Francisco: Jossey-Bass, 2010.

Cranton, P., and Taylor, E. (eds.), *The Handbook of Transformative Learning Theory.* San Francisco: Jossey-Bass, forthcoming.

Habermas, J. *Communication and the Evolution of Society.* Boston: Beacon Press, 1979.

National Institute of Mental Health."The Numbers Count: Mental Disorders in America," n.d. www.nimh.nih.gov/health/publications/the-numbers-count-mental-disorders-in-america/index.shtml.

STEPHEN BROOKFIELD *holds the title of distinguished university professor at the University of St. Thomas, Minneapolis-St. Paul, Minnesota.*

New Directions for Adult and Continuing Education • DOI: 10.1002/ace

5

Within dominant U.S. popular and psychiatric culture, adults who experience more than one distinct consciousness—that is, those who experience alterity, or the presence of "alters" or other personalities—are often pathologized as suffering from dissociative identity disorder (formerly multiple personality disorder).

Alterity: Learning Polyvalent Selves, Resisting Disabling Notions of the Self

Wayland Walker

This chapter queries how one type of human difference—alterity, the experience of multiple distinct consciousnesses, or "alters," by one person—is pathologized in American culture. This experience is inscribed as a mental illness, labeled now as dissociative identity disorder (DID; American Psychiatric Association, 1994) and formerly known as multiple personality disorder (MPD; American Psychiatric Association, 1980). In this analysis, the notion of the modernist subject or self as a linear, cohesive, unitary consciousness is challenged as a method of suppressing difference. Alternative language is proposed for talking about the self. Those who experience alterity can be said to experience polyvalent selves. If a singular self is commonplace, then polyvalent selves are queer, unusual, different, and worthy of study because such difference represents a creative and dynamic uncertainty that cannot be easily suppressed, explained, or interpreted away by modernist institutions and theories. Utilizing a postmodern and public pedagogy framework, I analyzed cinematic texts that depicted alterity to identify messages in popular culture that might be disabling to adult learners who experience alterity. The films reviewed consistently depicted alters as distinct and separate entities who, despite inhabiting the same body, communicate with difficulty. They also usually depicted alterity as a diseased condition caused by trauma that must be remembered in order to heal a putatively shattered self.

Preface: Alterity Defined

As Hill and Davis (2009) noted, "Labels not only describe, they *inscribe*" (p. 187). Since this is a project grounded not in psychiatry or psychology

NEW DIRECTIONS FOR ADULT AND CONTINUING EDUCATION, no. 132, Winter 2011 © 2011 Wiley Periodicals, Inc.
Published online in Wiley Online Library (wileyonlinelibrary.com) • DOI: 10.1002/ace.430

but in adult learning theory, I begin by offering a new and decidedly non-clinical lexicon for the human phenomenon described in the definition of DID.

Alter:
An alter is a consciousness, or personality, that regularly inhabits a body, often with its own particular name, mannerisms, likes, dislikes, identity markers, and memories, which may include alternative personal histories and relationships. To qualify as an alter, there must, of course, be more than one such consciousness; otherwise an alter is simply a Self.

Alterity:
Alterity is a word I have employed (Walker, 2010) for the experience of alters or more than one consciousness within a single body. I am deploying this word as an alternative to the language used in psychiatric texts to create a type of patient, the "multiple" or "dissociative," and to suggest that some people might experience alterity without being defined by that experience. In using the word in this fashion, I am also breaking from the historical uses of the word, as an experience of the Other (Baudrillard and Guillaume, 2008; Hazell, 2009), and using it in a more literal sense, as the experience of the Other as inside, rather than outside, a person's body.

Polyvalent selves:
A person who experiences alterity can be said to experience polyvalent selves, or the presence of multiple selves, which are each to some degree stable and enduring.

Self:
When used with capital "S," I am referring to the modernist Self, which is assumed in modernist discourses (St. Pierre, 2000) to exist, as a naturalized condition, in all people and which can be discovered or allowed to emerge by natural processes.

Dissociative Identity Disorder

This chapter is an offshoot of a larger project, grounded in adult education's public pedagogy theoretical discourse (Sandlin, Schultz, and Burdick, 2010) and similar analyses of movies and television shows as pedagogical instruments (Wright and Sandlin, 2009). "As a form of public pedagogy, film combines entertainment and politics and . . . lays claim to public memory" (Giroux, 2002, p. 6). I am analyzing depictions of alterity in cinematic texts in order to explore the implications for adult learning when and if an adult learner experiences:

A. The presence of two or more distinct identities or personalities or personality states (each with its own relatively enduring pattern of perceiving, relating to and thinking about the environment and self).

B. At least two of these identities or personality states recurrently take control of the person's behavior.

C. Inability to recall important personal information that is too extensive to be explained by ordinary forgetfulness.

D. The disturbance is not due to the direct physiological effects of a substance . . . or a general medical condition. (American Psychiatric Association, 1994, p. 487)

In American culture, this person has been declared, by medical fiat, mentally ill. Interestingly, just as "homosexuals" were once declared mentally ill based on their status as subjects desiring members of the same sex, there is no requirement that hosting multiple selves must cause the person who experiences it some distress. The distress, and the diseased condition, is presumed.

Central to this phenomenon is the presence of alternate personalities, or "alters," which alternatively "take control" of a body. The label for this experience has been changed from multiple personality disorder (American Psychiatric Association, 1980) in previous psychiatric discourse. However, this change was made only to conform the diagnosis more closely to that of other mental illnesses and to assert that alters were not personalities but rather fragments of personalities (Hacking, 1995). This language subordinates the human experience of alterity to that of illness by denying these "fragments" their personhood.

The certainty regarding the self created by these discourses—that there is one self in each human body, that this self fractures or multiplies in predictable ways—has led to a proliferation of books regarding the subject. Former University of Georgia football hero Herschel Walker penned *Breaking Free: My Life with Dissociative Identity Disorder* (Walker, Brozek, and Maxfield, 2008), describing how Christianity and psychology enabled him to gain control over his mental illness. Other books relate the heroic efforts of doctors in treating DID (Baer, 2007; Schreiber, 1973), and still others urge readers with DID "to accept your diagnosis, to work with your alter personalities, and to seek help if you are not already in therapy" (Mungadze, 2008, p. xviii). Mental health professionals warn that there is a hidden epidemic of dissociative disorders (Steinberg and Schnall, 2001), while self-identified dissociatives provide self-help manuals for living with the disorder (A.T.W., 2005).

Other Explanations for Alterity

This project began with an axiom: Some adult learners experience alterity, and this literal fracturing of the presumed Self has tremendous implications for how those individuals grow, navigate their lifeworlds, and engage in lifelong learning. There is an anthropological adage that human experiences marginalized as deviant in one culture can be honored in another. "Normality is not an objective given from which unproblematic behavioral assessments can be rendered independent of historical era, culture, subculture, or social group" (Bartholomew, 2000, p. 3). The human experience of alterity is no exception.

In many cultures, alterity takes the form of possession trance, which occurs when an alter, deemed a god, an ancestor, or spirit, assumes control of a person's body. "In Bali, ritual possession is common, controlled, desirable, socially useful, highly valued, positively reinforced by society, and individually satisfying" (Suryani and Jensen, 1993, pp. 45–46). The Balinese studied by Suryani and Jensen socialized the experience of alterity, and the authors concluded that "the fact that there are a number of phenomenological differences noted between MPD [alterity] and possession in the Balinese . . . does not detract from the hypothesis that both represent fundamentally the same psycho-biological process" (p. 214).

Indeed, the experience of alterity as possession by spirits in other cultures may contradict and refute Western dualism inherent in the concepts of self and even of spirit (Willis, 1999).

Contrary explanations for alterity were also once present in Western discourse. One classic method of social control is to erase alternative explanations from history. When the "true" story outline in the movie *The Three Faces of Eve* (Johnson, 1957) and its corollary psychiatric monograph (Thigpen and Cleckley, 1957) were published, the case of Eve was thought to be the only case of MPD in existence at that time (North, Ryall, Ricci, and Wetzel, 1993). There had, however, been an "epidemic" of MPD diagnoses at the end of the nineteenth century (Shamdasani, 1899/1994, p. xxxi). This epidemic was associated with spiritualism and mediumship, which included possession trance by alters—the same spiritualist movement that Braude (2001) has argued was an important component of the women's rights movement in the nineteenth century. Mediums, who were usually women, were regularly possessed by spirits, and during that epoch "the medical attack on mediums was a special case . . . of the medical attack on women in general. Doctors who viewed the female organization [the spiritualist movement] as inherently pathological saw mediums . . . as prime examples of pathology" (p. 157).

Such spiritual explanations for alterity arguably linger in New Age spirituality and trance channeling (Brown, 1997). Yet, despite this history, the psychiatric explanation of alterity—that it is always a diseased condition—remains hegemonic in popular culture and in adult educational theory on the self and learning.

Alterity Matters: The Theoretical Importance of the Self

There is not simply a heterosexual matrix (Butler, 1990/2006) constraining affectional expressions within its matrix grid of regularity and binaries of control. There is also a matrix that demands that each learner produce her- or himself as someone with an essence, someone with a coherent and knowable Self, which is necessary to achieve the favored status of authenticity (Carusetta and Cranton, 2005) and continuous personal growth (Rogers, 1979).

Other poststructuralist scholars have flirted with the notion of the fractured subject (Tierney, 2001), the subverted subject (Rosenau, 1992), the subject that is neither fixed nor stable but articulated in discourse (Honan, 2007), the self as a fiction inscribed by discourse (St. Pierre, 2000), and the self as a sort of wounded entity that can be freed by discourse (Jackson, 2003; Talburt and Rassmusen, 2010). Clark and Dirkx (2000) postulated that the unitary self is a construct that must be interrogated as the "Big Enchilada," which is "foundational to how we think about and theorize learning and a lot of other things—everything, in fact, that we care about as adult educators" (p. 101)—though these scholars appear more intent on breaking the unitary self into parts than in theorizing the possibility of multiple discrete but interconnected selves.

However, even the most radical of these knowledge-making projects, such as queer theory, too often succumb to the cultural imperative that the Self be made knowable and unified, even if that unity is paradoxically comprised only of an essential indeterminacy. "By accepting representational and transformational premises as fundamental to its purposes, queer research participates in producing the subjects on which liberalism (and neoliberalism) depends" (Talburt and Rasmussen, 2010, p. 7). In much academic discourse, then, the Self is a concept that resists reinterpretation or expansion. Alterity, as a human phenomenon, matters because its study challenges much existing thought on how adults learn, grow, and change.

Assuming that the experience of alters is a human experience that is mediated by culture and learning, this chapter explores notions in popular culture that, if believed true and acted on, create alterity as a disabling condition and a mental illness rather than a benign human difference. I do not contest that many people experiencing alterity may be experienced by others and themselves as mentally ill. I am questioning the deeply ingrained and peculiarly Western notion that, constitutionally, *all* adults who experience alterity are mentally ill.

Disabling Notions of the Self

For those who experience alterity, the effects of culture and learning may arguably be more profound, given the documented suggestibility of those who experience alters (Bliss, 1986). This population appears to be psychologically vulnerable. The definition of DID, given earlier, does not require distress. The distress is presumed in the diagnosis. Since those who experience alterity in other cultures do not always experience this distress (Suryani and Jensen, 1993), it must be to some extent learned.

New Directions for Adult and Continuing Education • DOI: 10.1002/ace

This analysis has identified two key disabling messages within popular depictions of alterity. These notions include (1) that alters must be discrete and self-contained, and so have difficulty communicating, and (2) that alterity is invariably created by trauma.

Alters as Discrete, Autonomous, and Conflicted

In all of the cinematic texts analyzed for this project, the characters experience their alters as discrete, autonomous selves. This is true even as alterity may transgress social norms and the history and reality of the character's body, as a protagonist experiencing alterity might have alters that profess different ages, different sexual orientations, different social classes, and even different genders. Dominant discourse on the Self requires that multiple selves remain separate and unique until they can be unified into a single, unique, and enduring Self. Alterity must be placed within a modernist psychiatric grid that can, for example, diagram with boxes and arrows the personalities of the protagonist in *The Three Faces of Eve* (Johnson, 1957) as measurable entities that change over time (Osgood and Luria, 1957). Each Self must be represented as "an essentially abstract entity, the 'monological self,' the self-contained individual having no transactions with and unaffected by anything 'other' to itself" (Usher, Bryant, and Johnston, 1997, p. 94).

This is an unusual message to send regarding alters, which, after all, inhabit the same body and must perforce share experiences and sensations. This complete separation and autonomy is also demonstrably false, because in every cinematic text, the alters experience co-consciousness or copresence. However, by conceptualizing each alter as discrete and self-contained, arguably memory lapses become inevitable and the adult learner spends much time in a perplexed state, compensating for those lapses and discontinuities. People forget all the time; for those diagnosed with DID, these lapses are presumed pregnant with meaning. Further, since "co-consciousness" of alters, or the experience of multiple alters at the same time, is possible, this division into discrete and isolated selves is not universal and may be learned or imposed. The public pedagogy of these films emphasizes the discrete nature of the alters and their difficulties in communicating with one another rather than the occasions in which alters cooperate toward common goals.

Alterity as the Product of Trauma

While other cultures might explain alterity as the product of spiritual forces and events, Western psychology requires that alterity be a diseased state created by trauma. Indeed, Acocella (1999) argues that after the movie *Sybil* (Petrie and Babbin, 1976), MPD "now had a clear cause: childhood abuse" (p. 3). In popular depictions of alterity, alters must be identified so that they

New Directions for Adult and Continuing Education • DOI: 10.1002/ace

can be merged into a single Self. Despite solid psychological research on memory that indicates that childhood sexual abuse is not processed or stored in a manner that would allow such recoveries (Clancy, 2009), that false memories of abuse can be created (Bjorklund, 2000; Loftus and Ketcham, 1994), and that the trauma myth damages patients (Ofshe and Watters, 1994), this merger continues to be the imposed treatment of choice for many adults experiencing alterity. Turkus and Kahler (2006) thus write that they deploy "psychoeducational" interventions in order to assist patients in "understanding the patients' experiences as normal human responses to trauma and how it disrupts one's life" (p. 246). The trauma is assumed and treated on the basis of the presenting symptom, the fractured or multiple Self.

This theory, that abuse always causes the experience of alterity, has become such a certainty that Ross (1989) admonishes therapists to remember that "the personality system . . . is driven by pain" (p. 109) and that therapists look for extreme abuse to explain the creation of what is always labeled a disorder. It is psychiatric canon that "[e]ffective treatment of MPD requires an understanding of its traumatic precipitants and the initially adaptive role of dissociation in mitigating overwhelming trauma during childhood" (Putnam, 1989, p. 45). Indeed, more contemporary accounts of DID report that it was caused by more extreme forms of abuse, including abuse by Satanic cultists (Mayer, 1991; Ofshe and Watters, 1994).

Imagine an adult learner who experiences alterity and has no grounding in postmodernist, feminist, and queer theory—that is, who has not considered the "disciplinary power" of psychiatric discourse that "functions through networks and the visibility of which is only found in the obedience and submission of those on whom it is silently exercised" (Foucault, 2003/2006, p. 22). Upon viewing such films, our imagined learner will likely perceive alterity as a disease and either hide such a condition or seek treatment from a therapist who will reinforce the idea that alterity is always an illness. Such a quest for traumatic roots in all people who experience alterity is likely to be, in itself, disabling, time consuming, and incredibly disruptive to family systems as "recovered memories" of decades-old abuse suddenly appear.

Conclusion

I began this chapter with the observation that many people experience alterity, which is currently either constrained as a mental illness and a reprehensible state or dismissed as a false illness and imaginary condition. "Skeptics contend that unlike disorders such as schizophrenia and mental retardation, [MPD] has no medical validity, and that it is more properly viewed as a social identity, often constructed as a joint effort of patients and their therapists" (Nathan and Snedeker, 2001, p. 48). Within dominant discourses, people who experience alterity face a binary choice: They are either mentally ill, or their condition is a fabrication and neither real nor true.

But we, as a culture, would not create so many cultural texts about a subject if it were not in some fashion collectively intriguing. Just as people were gay even when homosexuality was illegal, people clearly and repeatedly do report that they experience alterity, and many others are eager to view cinematic depictions of this human difference. This chapter has begun the process of thinking about alterity differently. This work suggests that perhaps some adult learners can forgo the psychological torture of recovering memories of trauma in favor of more fulfilling pursuits.

As a work of postmodernism as resistance (Britton, 1996), this chapter has sought to outline a few of the ways in which the grand ideology of the self limits the experience of alterity as a disabling event. It is a prelude to larger questions about identity and learning: If learners can legitimately experience disjunctures in their experience, if they can learn in radically new ways and are not constrained by the theoretical word prison of the presumed self, what new sorts of learning opportunities might be possible? Those who experience alterity are depicted as having at least one alter with specialized, almost superhuman abilities to learn new skills rapidly, to create art, to speak other languages, or to effectively manipulate social systems. What extraordinary feats of learning and human accomplishment might alterity facilitate? Finally, there is apparent in these movies a deep and abiding and peculiarly American terror of those who experience alterity. Further research must explore why.

References

Acocella, J. *Creating Hysteria: Women and Multiple Personality Disorder*. San Francisco: Jossey-Bass, 1999.

American Psychiatric Association. *Diagnostic and Statistical Manual of Mental Disorders*, 4th ed. Washington, D.C.: American Psychiatric Association, 1994.

American Psychiatric Association. *Diagnostic and Statistical Manual of Mental Disorders*, 3rd ed. Washington, D.C.: American Psychiatric Association, 1980.

A.T.W. *Got Parts? An Insider's Guide to Managing Life Successfully with Dissociative Identity Disorder*. Ann Arbor, Mich.: Loving Healing Press, 2005.

Baer, R. Switching Time: *A Doctor's Harrowing Story of Treating a Woman with 17 Personalities*. New York: Three Rivers Press, 2007.

Bartholomew, R. E. *Exotic Deviance: Medicalizing Cultural Idioms—From Strangeness to Illness*. Boulder: University of Colorado Press, 2000.

Baudrillard, J., and Guillaume, M. *Radical Alterity*. Trans. A. Hodges. Los Angeles: Semiotext(e), 2008.

Bjorklund, D. F. (ed.), *False-Memory Creation in Children and Adults*. Mahwan, N.J.: Lawrence Erlbaum, 2000.

Bliss, E. L. *Multiple Personality, Allied Disorders, and Hypnosis*. New York: Oxford University Press, 1986.

Braude, A. *Radical Spirits: Spiritualism and Women's Rights in Nineteenth-Century America*, 2nd ed. Bloomington: Indiana University Press, 2001.

Britton, D. *The Modern Practice of Adult Education: A Post-Modern Critique*. New York: State University of New York Press, 1996.

Brown, M. F. *The Channeling Zone: American Spirituality in an Anxious Age*. Cambridge, Mass.: Harvard University Press, 1997.

Butler, J. *Gender Trouble*. New York: Routledge, 2006. (Originally published 1990.)

Carusetta, E., and Cranton, P. "Nurturing Authenticity: A Conversation with Teachers." *Teaching in Higher Education*, 2005, *10*(3), 285–297.

Clancy, S. A. *The Trauma Myth: The Truth About the Sexual Abuse of Children—and Its Aftermath*. New York: Basic Books, 2009.

Clark, M. C., and Dirkx, J. M. "Moving Beyond a Unitary Self: A Reflective Dialogue." In A. L. Wilson and E. R. Hayes (eds.), *Handbook of Adult and Continuing Education*, new ed. San Francisco: Jossey-Bass, 2000.

Foucault, M. *Psychiatric Power: Lectures at the College de France, 1973–1974*. Graham Burchell, trans. New York: Picador, 2006. (Originally published 2003.)

Giroux, H. A. *Breaking In to the Movies: Film and the Culture of Politics*. Madden, Mass.: Blackwell, 2002.

Hacking, I. *Rewriting the Soul: Multiple Personalities and the Science of Memory*. Princeton, N.J.: Princeton University Press, 1995.

Hazell, C. *Alterity: The Experience of the Other*. Bloomington, Ind.: AuthorHouse, 2009.

Hill, R. J., and Davis, D. D. "Transsexuality: Challenging the Institutionalized Sex/Gender Binary." In R. J. Hill and A. P. Grace (eds.), *Adult and Higher Education in Queer Contexts: Power, Politics and Pedagogy*. Chicago: Discovery Association, 2009.

Honan, E. "Writing a Rhizome: An (Im)Plausible Methodology." *International Journal of Qualitative Studies in Education*, 2007, *20*(5), 531–546.

Jackson, A. Y. "Rhizovocality." *International Journal of Qualitative Studies in Education*, 2003, *16*, 693–710.

Johnson, N. (producer and director), *The Three Faces of Eve*. Los Angeles: 20th Century Fox, 1957. Film.

Loftus, E., and Ketcham, K. *The Myth of Repressed Memory: False Memories and Allegations of Sexual Abuse*. New York: St. Martin's Press, 1994.

Mayer, R. S. *Satan's Children: Case Studies in Multiple Personality*. New York: G. P. Putnam's Sons, 1991.

Mungadze, J. "Foreword from Dr. Jeff Mungadze." In H. Walker, G. Brozek, and C. Maxfield, *Breaking Free: My Life with Dissociative Identity Disorder*. New York: Howard Books, 2008.

Nathan, D., and Snedeker, M. *Satan's Silences: Ritual Abuse and the Making of a Modern American Witch Hunt*. Lincoln, NE: Authors Choice Press, 2001.

North, C. S., Ryall, J. M., Ricci, D. A., and Wetzel, R. D. *Multiple Personalities, Multiple Disorders: Psychiatric Classification and Media Influence*. New York: Oxford University Press, 1993.

Ofshe, R., and Watters, E. *Making Monsters: False Memories, Psychotherapy, and Sexual Hysteria*. New York: Charles Scribner's Sons, 1994.

Osgood, C. E., and Luria, Z. "Case Report: A Blind Analysis of a Case of Multiple Personality Using the Semantic Differential." In C. H. Thigpen and H. M. Cleckley, *The Three Faces of Eve*. New York: McGraw-Hill, 1957.

Petrie, D. (director), and Babbin, J. (producer), *Sybil*. New York: NBC, 1976. Film.

Putnam, F. W. *Diagnosis and Treatment of Multiple Personality Disorder*. New York: Guilford Press, 1989.

Rogers, C. *Freedom to Learn*. Columbus, OH: Charles E. Merrill, 1979.

Rosenau, P. M. *Post-Modernism and the Social Sciences: Insights, Inroads, and Intrusions*. Princeton, N.J.: Princeton University Press, 1992.

Ross, C. A. *Multiple Personality Disorder: Diagnosis, Clinical Features, and Treatment.* New York: John Wiley & Sons, 1989.

Sandlin, J. A., Schulz, B. D., and Burdick, J. "Understanding, Mapping and Exploring the Terrain of Public Pedagogy." In J. A. Sandlin, B. D. Schultz, and J. Burdick (eds.), *Handbook of Public Pedagogy: Exploring and Learning Beyond Schooling.* New York: Routledge, 2010.

Schreiber, F. R. *Sybil.* New York: Grand Central Publishing, 1973.

Shamdasani, S. "Introduction: Encountering Helene: Theodore Fournoy and the Genesis of Subliminal Psychology." In T. Flournoy, *From India to the Planet Mars: A Case of Multiple Personality with Imaginary Languages.* Trans. D. B. Vermilye. Princeton, N.J.: Princeton University Press, 1994. (Originally published 1899.)

Steinberg, M., and Schnall, M. *The Stranger in the Mirror: Dissociation—the Hidden Epidemic.* New York: Harper, 2001.

St. Pierre, E. A. "Poststructural Feminism in Education: An Overview." *International Journal of Qualitative Studies in Education,* 2000, *13,* 477–515.

Suryani, L. K., and Jensen, G. D. *Trance and Possession in Bali: A Window on Western Multiple Personality, Possession Disorder, and Suicide.* New York: Oxford University Press, 1993.

Talburt, S., and Rasmussen, M. L. "'After-Queer' Tendencies in Queer Research." *International Journal of Qualitative Studies in Education,* 2010, 23(1), 1–14.

Thigpen, C. H., and Cleckley, H. M. *The Three Faces of Eve.* New York: McGraw-Hill, 1957.

Tierney, W. G. "The Autonomy of Knowledge and the Decline of the Subject: Postmodernism and the Reformulation of the University." *Higher Education,* 2001, *41,* 353–372.

Turkus, J. A., and Kahler, J. A. "Therapeutic Interventions in Treatment of Dissociative Disorders." *Psychiatric Clinics of North American,* 2006, 29(1), 245–262.

Usher, R., Bryant, I., and Johnston, R. (1997). *Adult Education and the Postmodern Challenge: Learning Beyond the Limits.* New York: Routledge.

Walker, H., Brozek, G., and Maxfield, C. *Breaking Free: My Life with Dissociative Identity Disorder.* New York: Howard Books, 2008.

Walker, W. "Alterity: Queering the Monadic Self." Preconference paper presented at the CSSE Queer Conference, May 28, 2010, Montreal, Canada.

Willis, R. *Some Spirits Heal, Others Only Dance.* New York: Berg, 1999.

Wright, R. R., and Sandlin, J. A. "Cult TV, Hip Hop, Shape-Shifters, and Vampire Slayers: A Review of the Literature at the Intersection of Adult Education and Popular Culture." *Adult Education Quarterly,* 2009, 59(2), 118–141.

WAYLAND WALKER *is an attorney in private practice holding advanced degrees in law, psychology, anthropology, and health promotion and behavior. This chapter is an offshoot of his work toward a Ph.D. in adult education at the University of Georgia in Athens.*

After diagnosis of a child's disability, the parent adapts to the situation by learning how to best optimize the child's learning and development, despite the disability. However, often parents are overwhelmed because many feel ill equipped to deal with the realities of handling the child's physical, psychological, and/or educational needs.

6

Learning and Adaptation After Diagnosis: The Role of Parent Education

Thomas G. Reio, Jr., Sandra L. Fornes

Raising a child has its frustrating moments; parenting a child with special needs multiplies those times, and parents often experience high levels of stress and frustration (Hill, 2001; Smith, Oliver, and Innocenti, 2001). Parents are frequently overwhelmed when raising a child with a disability because many feel ill equipped to deal with the realities of effectively handling the child's physical, psychological, and/or educational needs. In addition, children with developmental disabilities are more likely than children without disabilities to develop behavior problems, creating further parental stress and depression (Emerson, 2003). The combination of a child with a disability and this parental stress may contribute to a continual pattern of problem behavior that can be mediated by positive parenting behaviors (Brookman-Frazee and Koegel, 2004; Deater-Deckard, 1998). The implementation of prevention and early intervention strategies is critical in providing parents the skills necessary to overcome and correct the early childhood difficulties and manage parental stress (Mahoney and others, 1999; McIntyre and Phaneuf, 2007).

Through parent education, parents learn to better recognize and deal productively with their child's physical, psychological, and educational needs (Mahoney and others, 1999). Thus, parental involvement and searching for information about specific ways to help their child's development is critical for fostering optimal developmental and behavioral outcomes for the child (Hill, 2001). Participation in parent education programs can be an integral part of parenting a child with special needs because it can provide

New Directions for Adult and Continuing Education, no. 132, Winter 2011 © 2011 Wiley Periodicals, Inc.
Published online in Wiley Online Library (wileyonlinelibrary.com) • DOI: 10.1002/ace.431

parents with the information and training needed to improve parenting skills and help moderate stress and frustration (McIntyre and Phaneuf, 2007). Indeed, the more parents understand about their child's needs and how those needs interact with the cognitive, social, emotional, and physical stages of child development, the easier and less stressful parenting can be (Shumow, 1998).

Effective parent education and family interventions lead to positive outcomes for both parents and children by reducing negative child–parent interactions and subsequent behavioral problems and increasing positive interactions (Lundahl, Risser, and Lovejoy, 2006). For parents of typically developing children, there is a vast amount of parent education literature to draw on for supporting the parent's informational, emotional, and social needs for the duration of his or her learning journey. For instance, Shumow (1998) found that participation in a parent education program improved parents' understanding of their children's reasoning and problem-solving skills and how best to foster both. As the parents acquired more information, their concerns decreased, their satisfaction increased, and they demonstrated an ability to transfer their learning to new situations. However, there exists limited literature regarding parent education for children with various special needs (Mahoney and others, 1999). Even less literature exists that deals specifically with special needs children in culturally diverse families (Santarelli, Koegel, Casas, and Koegel, 2001). This lack of literature and system supports (that is, educational and community systems) can add greatly to a parent's frustration (Brookman-Frazee and Koegel, 2004; Hill, 2001).

One author, Sandra, found frustration with the educational systems. It took months of distressing and investigating to realize that her son with special needs was not developing in the environment that the educational system felt was appropriate. Sandra noted:

> You soon realize that every child with special needs is very individualistic and there is no one prescription that will solve every child's situation. Children with special needs are grouped into categories and often the child is placed in an environment that doesn't work for him, providing further parental stress and frustration.

The other author, Tom, was frustrated by the shocking lack of guidance provided by physicians about what precisely his daughter's diagnosis was and the short- and long-term implications for her development. Besides a trifold pamphlet, no additional information was provided. Thus, it quickly became apparent that as a parent he was essentially on his own.

In this chapter, the authors explore the challenges of parenting a child with special needs and the trials and errors of finding appropriate skills to assist in their children's development and education. The authors begin with a brief introduction of ecocultural theory, followed by a presentation of parent education as it relates to children with special needs, including a discussion of parent empowerment. They conclude by offering suggestions and strategies for parenting children with special needs.

Parent Education

Ecocultural theory provides a comprehensive framework for working with families of children with disabilities (Gallimore, Goldenberg, and Weisner, 1993). Ecocultural niche, daily routines, and family accommodations are the main components of ecocultural theory (Gallimore, Goldenberg, and Weisner, 1993). Interventions should fit into the daily routines of a family and incorporate the goals and meaning that the family places on such routines. Ecocultural theory firmly supports expert parent education practice because it honors the roles not only of the child or parent but all the relevant stakeholders in the context of developing the special needs child.

Parent education is the process of providing parents with specific knowledge and systematic activities with the goal of promoting the development and competence of their children (Mahoney and others, 1999). Participation in parent education programs increases positive affect and behaviors in children and reduces parental stress (Koegel, Bimbela, and Schreibman, 1996). Through parent education, where the primary focus is on instructing the parent rather than socially supporting or encouraging him or her (encouragement and support do occur but are not the primary function), parents' ineffective parenting techniques are reduced and positive skills are increased. In typical programs, parents are taught strategies to assist children in performing developmentally appropriate cognitive and physical skills, managing behavior in daily routines, and interacting positively (Mahoney and others, 1999).

Historically speaking, however, early interventions with special needs children focused mostly on the child, with parents being almost superfluous to the child's learning and development and treatment. In this model, professionals were seen as being the one source of knowledge, and parents were not seen as active and equal partners. Thus, professionals did not see parents as co-collaborators in implementing strategies to facilitate the development of the child (Mahoney and others, 1999). More recent family support models, where family services and coping resources are emphasized, also underestimate the role of the parent in the child's development. In the family support models, parental effectiveness at meeting their child's developmental needs is seen as being a function of their psychological and socioeconomic well-being, with parental knowledge of child rearing and development as being of secondary import (Mahoney and others, 1999). Research into the efficacy of such family support models remains mixed, but there is evidence that parent-implemented interventions (that is, parents taught intervention strategies) can be superior to therapist-led family support over time (for example, Kaiser, Hancock, and Hester, 1998). Current researchers advocate including parental education as an integral part of the overall strategy to nurture children, especially those with special needs (Brookman-Frazee and Koegel, 2004; McIntyre and Phaneuf, 2007).

Because parent education is designed to supply *parents* with the specific knowledge and systematic activities needed to promote the optimal development of the child (Mahoney and others, 1999), caution must be exercised when considering children with special needs. Each special needs child has diverse, distinctive needs, and the specific knowledge and systematic activities related to one child should not be generalized to another. We must be mindful also that the intensity of activity related to an intervention will differ by child, again determined by need. Programs that balance the child's needs and intervention intensity with the needs of the family may be especially beneficial (Warren, Fey, and Yoder, 2007).

Mahoney and others (1999) highlighted the importance of a more self-directed approach to parent education as part of an overall strategy to working with professionals in meeting the child's specific needs. They argued that parent education must include the knowledge and skills parents acquire through their own learning and experience because it allows them to more completely mediate parenting the child with special needs.

Both authors followed a self-directed learning approach in dealing with their respective situations and in parenting their child. Self-directed learning is a process in which individuals take the initiative to diagnose learning needs, formulate learning goals, identify resources for learning, select and implement learning strategies, and evaluate learning outcomes (Knowles, 1975). The authors observed:

> After my daughter's diagnosis, it was pretty clear we were at the beginning of a learning journey, as we were almost completely on our own to find more information about her disability, learn how to be more responsive parents to her needs, be an advocate for her as appropriate at school, locate support groups if needed, etc. Still, we didn't join support groups or any of the like. We chose, instead, to look at our daughter's situation as an opportunity to highlight her wonderful attributes and to foster optimalization of her perceived weaknesses, working productively to raise a pretty interesting young woman.

> It took months to convince the education system that my son was not developing in the environment that the educational system felt was appropriate. The mainstreamed school he attended provided only the necessary tools to integrate a child into the system, but failed to provide equipment, services, and learning opportunities to help his development and improve his functional abilities. For example, the system mandates every child to participate in physical education; however, my son was never able to participate since the school didn't have any specialized equipment to assist him in physical

education. The school offered no other recreational activities that could help him physically develop. In addition, the school provided very few tools and instruction to help meet my son's educational needs. We finally discovered a tool, multisensory stimulation, that not only improved his focus, but improved his learning ability, development, and quality of life. The multi-sensory environment proved to be critical to his gaining building-block skills and experiencing success.

While many self-directed learners attempt to gain new skills, knowl-edge, and attitudes to improve their work performance, others, such as the authors, conducted their self-directed learning for the purpose of improv-ing family life and health (Lowry, 1989). Both authors leaned heavily on the parent education literature to guide them in their efforts to understand how best to improve their family's quality of life and the health of their child. This type of self-directed learning leads to the development of parent empowerment (Brookman-Frazee and Koegel, 2004).

Parent Empowerment

Parent and family empowerment highlights effective parenting skills, knowl-edge, parent involvement, and self-efficacy. This empowerment builds a col-laborative relationship between parent and professional, positively affecting the parent–child interaction (Brookman-Frazee and Koegel, 2004). Parent empowerment as positive self-judgments and parental self-efficacy focuses beyond the individual and the parent–child context. Empowerment includes a willingness to learn new parenting skills and become active in the child's treatment program, community resources, and political system. Parent empowerment enables parents to become collaborators in their child's inter-vention and educational plan (Scheel and Rieckmann, 1998). Empower-ment models of interventions enable parents and families to acquire competencies to solve problems, meet their child's needs, and attain family goals. Empowered parents demonstrate lower levels of stress, higher self-efficacy, and higher levels of confidence, which lead to greater child out-comes and increased generalization of treatment gains (Koegel, Bimbela, and Schreibman, 1996).

Parent empowerment suggests that parents should take an active role not only in implementing the intervention but also in developing an inter-vention that will fit into the family's daily routine (Brookman-Frazee and Koegel, 2004). The parent is considered the expert on his or her own child and takes responsibility for deciding how procedures will be imple-mented and incorporated into the family's daily routines. This autonomy can minimize stress and frustration by educating the parent about his or her child's problem and becoming a knowledgeable and forceful advocate for the child. To be sure, the more the parent knows, the more empowered he or she will feel. What is more, the parent will be able to ask more intelligent questions, better evaluate answers and recommendations, and pursue solutions that are likely to help his or her child (Brookman-Frazee and Koegel, 2004).

Through parent empowerment, one author created an environment that would enhance her son's ability to learn through a technique of multisensory simulation and developed a multisensory environment to help her son learn and develop. A multisensory environment is designed to promote neurological activity and to encourage relaxation. Such an environment is a dedicated space or room where sensory stimulation can be controlled (intensified or reduced); presented in isolation or combination; packaged for active or passive interactions; and matched to fit the perceived motivation, interests, and/or educational needs of the user. Well-chosen, controlled multisensory stimuli for children with neurological challenges and those withdrawn from their environment help promote development, learning, improved communication and positively affect behavior, leading to improved learning, happiness, and quality of life (Hidden Angel Foundation, 2010).

The other author was able to use parent empowerment to create a home environment where his daughter could develop her physical and spatial skills far beyond what might be expected with someone with her disability. The entire basement and her bedroom were set up with a number of what she perceived to be fun but rigorous physical activities where she could work to strengthen her physical condition and unknowingly develop her spatial skills (for example, hand coordination, balance, aiming and hitting a target). Because the basement and bedroom activities were set up to be fun rather than a chore, she willingly worked daily to improve. These activities promoted a strong sense of self where her confidence carried her to becoming a member of both track and tennis teams.

While children of empowered parents demonstrate more positive affect (happiness and interest), higher levels of responding, and appropriate engagement (Brookman-Frazee and Koegel, 2004), there are other strategies to be mindful of when parenting a child with special needs.

Other Strategies

While each parent gains knowledge and confidence through parent empowerment, in this section we provide additional parent education strategies for parenting children with special needs.

McIntyre and Phaneuf (2007) suggest a three-tier approach to parent education that includes: self-administered reading materials; group-based parent education; and individualized sessions that involve direct techniques, practice, feedback, and reinforcement. Self-administered parent education provides parents with literature, audiovisual material, or computer-delivered information (McIntyre and Phaneuf, 2007) and has been shown to be as effective as professional-directed, individually administered programs (Markie-Dadds and Sanders, 2006). Group-based programs allow families to receive more professional attention than the self-administered format. The collateral benefit and peer support of group programs may increase parental engagement (Webster-Stratton, 2001). This peer support has a positive impact on children's cognitive outcomes, strengthens family bonds, and gives parents an opportunity to share experience. Individually administered programs, where individual sessions are provided by a professional, increase flexibility and can be tailored to the specific situation (McIntyre and Phaneuf, 2007). The individual approach was found to be more effective when serving families with specific needs (Lundahl, Risser, and Lovejoy, 2006). Individualized supports are provided to parents in a natural environment and focus on specific areas of difficulties, such as behavior management, developmentally appropriate social skills, or other content areas (McIntyre and Phaneuf, 2007).

Parent empowerment where parents mediate the intervention is compatible with a family-centered approach to early intervention and parental education programs. The family-centered approach provides for collaboration with the parents and families (Mahoney and others, 1999). Promoting family relationships is a key component. Increasing positive parent–child interactions has been found to enhance parenting behaviors. Father involvement in parent training leads to better outcomes and promotes family cooperation and cohesion (Lundahl, Tollefson, Risser, and Lovejoy, 2008). Because children with disabilities and their families often experience additional risk factors, they benefit from intervention services that support both the child and family functioning (McIntyre and Phaneuf, 2007). With regard to family function, lack of family resources and family support are strong predictors of overall parenting stress. Family education programs should focus on family strengths and resiliencies rather than family weaknesses (Mahoney and others, 1999). Analysis of a family's activities and daily routines provides a window into the family's ecology and is an essential component in the development of family support programs (Gallimore and others, 1993). Family-centered parent education includes family skill training and family activities to assist children and their parents to communicate effectively and take advantage of concrete social supports.

Conclusion

In conclusion, through parenting children with special needs, the authors found themselves on a self-directed learning journey where the information and learning acquired made them feel empowered to become active collaborators in the child's development. They both took the risk of stepping beyond the advice of well-meaning experts to experimenting with and creating new developmentally appropriate practices for the benefit of their child. We close by advocating a research agenda where parent education can be systematically investigated as an essential part of early interventions for special needs children. Phenomenological research could be designed to explore the self-directed parenting experience of working to meet the requirements of a special needs child. The self-directed parenting experience linked to empowerment within the context of families from understudied ethnic minorities should also be investigated. Researchers might also implement studies where self-directed approaches to parent education are compared to more traditional approaches with respect to meeting the clearly delineated short- and long-term needs of the child.

References

Brookman-Frazee, L., and Koegel, R. L. "Using Parent/Clinician Partnerships in Parent Education Programs for Children with Autism." *Journal of Positive Behavior Interventions*, 2004, 6(4), 195–213.

Deater-Deckard, K. "Parenting Stress and Child Adjustment: Some Old Hypotheses and New Questions." *Clinical Psychology: Science and Practice*, 1998, 5, 314–332.

Emerson, E. "Prevalence of Psychiatric Disorders in Children and Adolescents With and Without Intellectual Disabilities." *Journal of Intellectual Disability Research*, 2003, 47, 51–58.

Gallimore, R., Goldenberg, C. N., and Weisner, T. S. "The Social Construction and Subjective Reality of Activity Settings: Implications for Community Psychology." *American Journal of Community Psychology*, 1993, 21, 537–559.

Gallimore, R., and others. "Family responses to young children with developmental delays: Accommodation activities in ecological and cultural context." American Journal on Mental Retardation, 1993, 93(2), 185–206.

Hidden Angel Foundation. "Christopher Douglas Hidden Angel Foundation." n.d. [Brochure]. http://cdhaf.org/wp-content/uploads/2010/07/Brochure-vFinal.pdf.

Hill, L. H. "My Child Has a Learning Disability. Now What?" *Adult Learning*, 2001, 12, 24–25.

Kaiser, A. P., Hancock, T. B., and Hester, P. P. "Parents as Co-Interventionists: Research on Applications on Naturalistic Language Teaching Procedures." *Infants and Young Children*, 1998, 10, 1–11.

Knowles, M. *Self-Directed Learning: A Guide for Learners and Teachers.* New York: Association Press, 1975.

Koegel, R. L., Bimbela, A., and Schreibman, I. "Collateral Effects of Two Parent Training Programs on Family Interactions." *Journal of Autism and Developmental Disorders*, 1996, 26, 347–359.

Lowry, C. M. *Supporting and Facilitating Self-Directed Learning.* ERIC Digest No. 93. Columbus: ERIC Clearinghouse on Adult, Career, and Vocational Education, Ohio State University, 1989. www.ntlf.com/html/lib/bib/89dig.htm.

Lundahl, B., Risser, H. J., and Lovejoy, C. "A Meta-Analysis of Parent Training: Moderators and Follow-Up Effects." *Clinical Psychology Review*, 2006, 26, 86–104.

Lundahl, B., Tollefson, D., Risser, H., and Lovejoy, M. C. "A Meta-Analysis of Father Involvement in Parent Training." *Research on Social Work Practice*, 2008, 18, 97–106.

Mahoney, G., and others. "Parent Education in Early Intervention: A Call for a Renewed Focus." *Topics in Early Childhood Special* Education, 1999, 19(3), 131–140.

Markie-Dadds, C., and Sanders, M. R. "Self-Directed Triple P (Positive Parenting Programs) for Mothers with Children at Risk of Developing Conduct Problems." *Behavioral and Cognitive Psychotherapy*, 2006, 34, 259–275.

McIntyre, L. L., and Phaneuf, L. K. "A Three-Tier Model of Parent Education in Early Childhood." *Topics in Early Childhood Special Education*, 2007, 27(4), 214–222.

Santarelli, G., Koegel, R. L., Casas, J. M., and Koegel, L. K. "Culturally Diverse Families Participating in Behavior Therapy Parent Education Programs for Children with Developmental Disabilities." *Journal of Positive Behavior Interventions*, 2001, 3, 120–123.

Scheel, M. J., and Riechmann, T. "An Empirically Derived Description of Self-Efficacy and Empowerment for Parents of Children Identified as Psychologically Disordered." *American Journal of Family Therapy*, 1998, 26, 15–27.

Shumow, L. "Contributions of Parent Education to Adult Development." In M. C. Smith and T. Pourchot (eds.), *Adult Learning and Development: Perspectives from Educational Psychology*. Mahwah, NJ: Erlbaum, 1998.

Smith, T. B., Oliver, M. N. I., and Innocenti, M. S. "Parenting Stress in Families of Children with Disabilities." *American Journal of Orthopsychiatry Association*, 2001, 71(2), 257–261.

Warren, S. F., Fey, M. E., and Yoder, P. J. "Differential Treatment Intensity Research: A Missing Link to Creating Optimally Effective Communication Interventions." *Mental Retardation and Developmental Disabilities Research Review*, 2007, 12(1), 70–77.

Webster-Stratton, C. *The Incredible Years: Parents, Teachers, and Children Training Services: Leader's Guide*. Seattle, Wash.: Author, 2001.

THOMAS G. REIO, JR., is an associate professor in the Department of Leadership and Professional Studies at Florida International University, where he studies learning motivation, cognitive and sensory curiosity, risk taking, and workplace socialization. He is editor of Human Resource Development Review *and coeditor of* New Horizons in Adult Education *and* Human Resource Development.

SANDRA L. FORNES is executive director of Hidden Angel Foundation, Inc. in Birmingham, Alabama. The foundation exists to enrich the lives, health, and social well-being of people who are neurologically challenged through the use of multisensory stimulation.

7

As American communities welcome home U.S. troops from Iraq and Afghanistan, it is important to understand the unique set of circumstances for military personnel who served in these Middle Eastern regions. Differences in deployment, the type of injuries sustained, and the mixture of personnel continue to affect transitions from military service and reintegration into civilian life.

Challenges and Opportunities of Operation Enduring Freedom/ Operation Iraqi Freedom Veterans with Disabilities Transitioning into Learning and Workplace Environments

Fariba Ostovary, Janet Dapprich

The United States deployed more than 1.9 million troops to Afghanistan and Iraq since October 7, 2001, during two major military operations: Operation Enduring Freedom (OEF; October 2001–ongoing) and Operation Iraqi Freedom (OIF; March 2003–September 2010). These actions were part of the effort to pursue the U.S. global war on terrorism. As American communities welcome home U.S. troops from Iraq and Afghanistan, it is important to understand the unique set of circumstances for military personnel who served in these Middle Eastern regions. Differences in deployment, the type of injuries sustained, and the mixture of personnel continue to affect transitions from military service and reintegration into civilian life. Reintegration problems are measured by difficulties in areas of occupational, social integration, physical function, emotional well-being, and social functions (Resnik, Plow, and Jette, 2009). Transition into civilian employment and educational environments may be complicated for veterans who experience these difficulties, which often are misunderstood by the general population. According to Schlossberg, Waters, and Goodman (1995), "Transitions alter our lives—our roles, relationships, routines, and assumptions. . . . It is not the transition per se that is critical, but how much it changes one's roles, relationships, routines, and assumptions. The bigger the change, the greater

New Directions for Adult and Continuing Education, no. 132, Winter 2011 © 2011 Wiley Periodicals, Inc.
Published online in Wiley Online Library (wileyonlinelibrary.com) • DOI: 10.1002/ace.432

63

the potential impact and the longer it may take to incorporate the transition and move on" (pp. 2–3).

The war in Afghanistan, OEF, is the longest military conflict in U.S. history, spanning more than 10 years. The length of the OEF conflict combined with OIF created unique circumstances for the all-volunteer armed forces. Approximately 40 percent of men and women activated from the reserve component (approximately 12 percent) were deployed more than one time (Institute of Medicine, 2010). Increases in the frequencies and length of deployments and stressors associated with multiple exposures to combat areas create increased difficulties for reservists attempting to reintegrate into previous civilian roles in workforce or educational settings (Sargeant, 2009).

In 2005, female troops reached the highest numbers in U.S. military history, constituting 14 percent of the military workforce (Institute of Medicine, 2010). Under military regulations, women are precluded from direct combat, such as infantry, positions. However, since female troops performed duties in support positions as combat medics, military police, and convoy operations, female troops were exposed to dangers, consequences, and traumas of combat situations. Special problems reported by women veterans were higher rates of military sexual trauma and the mental health consequences related to this trauma (Street, Vogt, and Dutra, 2009). Additionally most of these women receive their comprehensive healthcare in a male-dominated environment where there may be little acknowledgment, understanding, or empathy of the new female veteran experience.

This chapter presents issues related to disabled military servicemen and women who are transitioning to civilian life. The emphasis is on the experience of veterans serving in the OEF and OIF as they reintegrate into civilian workplace and learning environments. We begin with an overview of the types of disabilities particular to these veterans and then describe the unique experiences of these disabled veterans in workplaces and institutions of higher education.

Today's medical service delivery and changes in armor technology increased the survival rate of injured OIF/OEF veterans (Goldberg, 2010). Veterans with polytrauma injuries, multiple injuries to one or more body regions or organs, have access to specialized polytrauma systems of care. These care systems provide treatment for physical, cognitive, psychological, and functional impairments and comprehensive and ongoing services for reintegration into educational and employment settings. This chapter focuses on the disabilities that may be more difficult to recognize and therefore might create areas of concern in higher education and workplace environments.

Posttraumatic stress disorder (PTSD) and neurological impairments (including traumatic brain injury [TBI]), often associated with polytrauma, are listed among the top four military service-related disabilities (U.S. Department of Veterans Affairs, 2010a). PTSD and TBI inherently include cognitive and psychological disabilities and are known as the signature wounds of OEF/OIF veterans (Institute of Medicine, 2010). Vasterling and others (2006) suggested that combat exposure alone may reduce proficiency in sustained attention and memory, including retention and recall, causing problems in educational and employment settings. These functional deficits impact daily functioning and require disability services under the Americans with Disabilities Act (Church, 2009). Daily stressors associated with transitioning into civilian life may involve lingering effects of combat experiences that interfere with veterans' abilities to acknowledge functional deficits or disabilities (Grossman, 2009; Holloway, 2009–2010; Sargeant, 2009).

An estimated 13.8 percent of OIF/OEF veterans experience symptoms of PTSD (Tanielian and Jaycox, 2008, p. 10). Symptoms such as hypervigilance, intrusive thoughts, severe anxiety, irritability, difficulty concentrating, and sensitivity to noise may interfere with educational and occupational functional requirements (American Psychiatric Association, 2000). These symptoms, sometimes viewed as odd or inappropriate behavior by the general public, can be viewed as a weakness by the veterans themselves. Individual pride, and/or the stigma of having a mental health diagnosis and the enhanced emotional suppression of the military culture, often leads to increased isolation (Hall, 2011). Isolation increases barriers and may lead to poor integration into social, educational, and occupational settings (Burnett and Segoria, 2009; Kim and others, 2010; Pietrzak and others, 2009).

Many combat veterans experience both PTSD and TBI symptoms. TBIs are sustained primarily from blast explosions, motor vehicle accidents, and gunshot wounds. The injuries and symptoms may be vague and vary in severity. Most mild TBI symptoms resolve in three to six months; however, symptoms may continue to develop into chronic postconcussive syndrome. Cognitive symptoms may include memory deficit, attention difficulties, and decrease in processing speed. Emotional difficulties, including irritability, depression, anxiety, impulsivity, and aggression, may overlap with symptoms of PTSD. Somatic symptoms of tinnitus, blurred vision, sensitivity to noise, seizures, and insomnia can worsen cognitive and emotional symptoms. The most common persistent symptoms are migraines, ranging from mild to severe headaches that can last more than four hours and can interfere with daily functioning (Tepe and Fendley, 2009; U.S. Department of Veterans Affairs, 2010a). For example, a veteran with a desk in a high-traffic, bright, and noisy area may experience increases in migraines and irritability, which may interfere with the concentration needed for employment or learning-related tasks. Veterans may choose to ignore or minimize PTSD/TBI symptoms, given the social stigma associated with mental health disorders and the desire to fit in with peers (Holloway, 2009–2010). Disclosure and the decision whether to disclose disabilities or not may be the single greatest challenge facing veterans transitioning into workplace and academic environments (Madaus, Miller, and Vance, 2009). Veterans with disabilities may benefit from accommodation and assistance, but without disclosure, they may not be able to access or may be ineligible for services allowable under law.

The Americans with Disabilities Act Amendments Act (ADAAA) shifts focus from whether a person has a disability to what employers or institutions should do to meet their obligation to provide equal opportunities and reasonable accommodations (Human Resources Focus Report, 2011). Grossman (2009) reports that new regulations under the ADAAA and large enrollments of veterans could converge to create a "perfect storm" effect on college and university campuses ill prepared to meet the needs and demands of the new era veterans.

Educational Environment

In higher education, veterans from previous combat eras have been identified as "catalysts" for changes in programs and services provided to persons with disabilities (Madaus, Miller, and Vance, 2009). The post–World War I era produced the Commission on National Aid to Vocational Education and the Disabled Veterans Act. These programs, followed by World War II's Servicemen's Readjustment Act and the Vietnam Era's Veteran's Readjustment Assistance Act, influenced services for all students with disabilities in post-secondary environments (Madaus, Miller, and Vance, 2009). U.S. colleges and universities are responding to the needs of the OEF/OIF-era veteran students with disabilities under the provisions of the ADAAA. The Equal Employment Opportunity Coalition provided the final interpretations on March 28, 2011 (Schuman and Hartstein, 2011).

Enrollment.   Currently OEF/OIF veteran enrollments at U.S. colleges and universities reflect the highest numbers since the post–World War II era, when the first military educational benefit assistance programs were legislated in 1944 (Cook and Kim, 2009; U.S. Department of Veterans Affairs, 2010b). The U.S. Department of Veterans Affairs Veterans Benefits Administration education assistance programs were designed to support educational or vocational opportunities missed because of military service (2010). The post 9/11 GI Bill, passed in 2008, provides tuition and fees, monthly housing allowance, books and supplies, and living expense stipends to eligible veterans. Only four months after benefits were made available in August 2009, this GI Bill accounted for 27.2 percent of the total student beneficiary population and amassed expenditures exceeding $500,000 (U.S. Department of Veterans Affairs, 2010b). The post 9/11 GI Bill benefits are not available at non-degree-granting institutions, apprenticeship programs, or on-the-job training programs. Housing allowances are not available for part-time students or for those only enrolled in online courses (American Council on Education, 2009; U.S. Department of Veterans Affairs, 2010b). Grossman (2009) reports that as many as 40 percent of veterans enrolling in postsecondary institutions may have some type of disability.

New Directions for Adult and Continuing Education • DOI: 10.1002/ace

Challenges. Financial security is consistently reported as a primary military enlistment rationale (DiRamio, Ackerman, and Mitchell, 2008). Following discharge from the military, OEF/OIF-disabled veterans identify that the loss of direct access to federal benefits and services available during their military service created barriers during the transition and reintegration into academic environments. The lengthy and complicated bureaucratic processes required by service organizations involved in disabled veterans' transitions may additionally become barriers to successful educational outcomes. The post 9/11 GI Bill mandates that eligibility for educational benefits must be declared early in the transition process and places time restrictions on the allocation of benefits. Accelerated enrollments may place veterans at risk to experience the onset of anger outbursts, poor concentration, and increased irritability when placed in stressful academic settings (Burnett and Segoria, 2009; DiRamio, Ackerman, and Mitchell, 2008). Crowded and noisy classroom settings heighten arousal, contributing to attention and concentration deficits. Special seating arrangements or requests to leave the classroom may be needed to relieve anxiety (Church, 2009). Veterans commonly report problems associated with academic demands, socialization with peers, and limited access to services in postsecondary institutions (DiRamio, Ackerman, and Mitchell, 2008). Efforts of the federal, state, and local agencies providing services to students with disabilities lack coordination and remains an area of concern (Dutta, Schiro-Geist, and Kundu, 2009; Shackleford, 2009).

Opportunities. Veteran-friendly campuses address the experiences and expectations of OEF/OIF students as they transition into U.S. colleges and universities. Veteran-friendly campuses strive for effective collaboration between all entities involved in the transition of the disabled veterans (Burnett and Segoria, 2009). Some examples of veteran-friendly campus actions include on-campus vet centers, orientation programs specifically designed for veterans, intramural sports programs and accessibility services for students with disabilities, and campus-wide interdepartmental committees on veteran services (Ackerman, DiRamio, and Mitchell, 2009). A "complete education" for these students blends school and real-world skills through the application of universal design process (Branker, 2009, p. 59). This universal design solves problems for end users and addresses the course experiences, expectations, and outcomes. An example of this is the Service Members Opportunity Colleges, a collaboration designed to improve transitions in and out of academic environments by streamlining matriculation, relocation, and reenrollment processes (Ford, Northrup, and Wiley, 2009).

Student veteran organizations (SVOs) were consistently reported as valuable entities providing supportive services to veterans, administrators, students, and staff. SVOs increase interactions with veterans and other students, provide mentoring programs and support, and provide source information to administrators, faculty, and students (Branker, 2009; Burnett and

Segoria, 2009; Holloway, 2009–2010; Madaus, Miller, and Vance, 2009). The University of Kansas SVO implemented programs and policies that allowed veterans to remain enrolled at the university despite delayed government tuition payments (Ford, Northrup, and Wiley, 2009). Indiana University's SVO guided by the School of Education developed and implemented a two-credit college course designed to improve understanding of the veteran combat and transition experience (Sumerlot, Green, and Parker, 2009). Given that combat operations in the Middle East are still underway, veteran service needs should remain a strategic imperative in both education and workplace environments (Ackerman, DiRamio, and Mitchell, 2009).

Work Environment

Loughran and Klerman (2008) noted that OIF/OEF veterans' unemployment rates increased by 58 percent from 2002 to 2005. OIF/OEF veterans transitioning from a military to civilian workforce adapt to environmental changes, such as physical work environment, reporting structure, job tasks, and relationships with others. The Department of Veterans Administration (VA) offers several programs designed to address unemployment and the vocational and rehabilitation needs of disabled veterans. The extent of benefits depends on the character of military discharge and the severity of the veteran's disability. OIF/OEF veterans must apply and be deemed qualified for benefits. Veterans overwhelmed by the amount and complexity of information available may not be aware of specific details of their benefits under current policies. Vocational rehabilitation professionals can help in navigating the many government agencies to obtain benefits and information and to develop strategies to attain education and employment. Employment services such as job training, employment-seeking skills, and résumé development are some of the services available to veterans. Under the VA, medical or psychiatric conditions related to or aggravated by the military service are considered "service-connected" disabilities, which entitles the veterans to monetary, increased health, and other benefits (U.S. Department of Veterans Affairs, 2011). Although most benefits offered are through the VA, other public, nonprofit, veteran service organizations and private agencies offer specific assistance to veterans.

   Vocational Rehabilitation. Vocational rehabilitation benefits are offered through two separate entities, the Veterans Health Administration and the Veterans Benefits Administration under the Department of Veterans Affairs. Although veterans with service-connected disabilities can access services through both entities, Veterans Health Administration institutions, known to many as VA hospitals, offer vocational rehabilitation benefits to veterans with or without service connection if a medical or psychiatric condition or barrier prevents educational and employment attainment. The ultimate goal of vocational rehabilitation is to prepare veterans to find and keep

New Directions for Adult and Continuing Education • DOI: 10.1002/ace

suitable employment. With guidance from vocational rehabilitation counselors, veterans in such programs set the highest realistic goals for employment and educational attainment. Some veterans benefit from setting short-term goals, such as dealing better with authority figures or modifying social skills for the civilian work environment. Disabled veterans may benefit from a variety of programs, including compensated work therapy and incentive work therapy. Supported employment and transitional work programs are the two major components of compensated work therapy, and services can be delivered in community, residential rehabilitation, and/or sheltered environment settings. These programs aim to transition veterans into the highest level of independent occupational functioning. Under the supported employment program and transitional work program, veterans are entitled to their service-connected disability income and income earned from their employment earnings. An unintended effect of disability compensation is discouraging full participation in vocational rehabilitation, resulting in lower number of hours worked (Drew and others, 2001). Vocational rehabilitation programs improve the likelihood of employment. Supported employment assists individuals with mental health diagnoses to increase their skills in a supportive environment (Ackerman and McReynolds, 2005). In studies of civilian populations with chronic mental illness and PTSD, it was found that having PTSD leads to lower rates of competitive employment, fewer hours worked, and less wages earned in clients participating in vocational rehabilitation (American Council on Education, 2009). Frueh, Henning, Pelligrin, and Choboth (1997) noted that combat veterans with PTSD and a higher intensity of anger symptoms were less likely to be employed. Effective treatment of PTSD improves the ability of veterans to benefit from supported employment (Mueser and others, 2004). Functional independence and return to work and/or school in younger veterans with TBI is improved when cognitive-didactic rehabilitation is used that emphasizes teaching learning skills, building self-awareness, and cognitive executive functions, such as working memory, mental tracking, functional communication, and self-awareness (Vanderploeg and others, 2008). Functional learning of specific skills, behaviors, compensation techniques, and task-specific checklists were more useful for older and more educated veterans with TBI. Burk and Degeneffe (2009) suggested a comprehensive rehabilitation approach to assist veterans with combination PTSD/TBI diagnosis. Specific recommendations for the community were increasing outreach programs to employers, educators, clergy, and other community leaders to increase awareness and provide information on useful resources.

Opportunities. The U.S. Department of Labor (2010) published guidelines for employer accommodation for veterans with PTSD and TBI. The guidelines advocate models of peer mentoring, group mentoring, and E-mentoring with a focus on achieving employment goals for both employer and the disabled employee. Special accommodation considerations for individuals with PTSD may include a flexible work schedule, schedule reminders, scheduled rest breaks, task checklists, and a low-noise environment. In addition to these accommodations, veterans with PTSD and TBI may benefit from adjusting expectations to complete tasks, limiting multitasking, using tape recorders as memory aids, and scheduling more difficult tasks at the beginning of the workday. The Department of Labor also provides training for institutions via online training, brochures with useful tips on accommodation, and connection with other sites that offer additional services for veterans.

The current recommendations for veterans with disabilities include vocational rehabilitation, treatment of underlying health issues, and modification of work and educational environment, with a recovery-focused model. Symptoms of PTSD, TBI, and chronic illnesses, such as pain, may fluctuate and may improve or subside entirely. For that reason, disabling symptoms and level of functioning may change over time. The appropriate level of assistance varies and needs to be adjusted if symptoms worsen or improve. Employers, educators, and other professionals may benefit from recognizing difficulties and referring the veterans to available resources.

Conclusion

This chapter highlights the process of transitioning veterans with PTSD/TBI into educational and employment environments. Some similarities exist in approaches to dealing with problems in both environments during the transition. Access to assistance, benefits, and agencies were identified as problematic. Collaboration among government, educational institutions, employers, and veterans provides overall positive outcomes when leaders, professors, employees, students, and the community at large are informed of the veterans' needs.

Gender-specific research studies are needed to examine the effects of readjustment on mothers and children separated during deployments and reintegration. Large multicenter studies and consistent research measures have not been established that investigate the transition from service to education or work or the effects of PSTD and TBI on the transition. Psychological effects of multiple deployments may need to be examined further for a more comprehensive understanding of the educational and employment reintegration needs of OEF/OIF veterans. Stigma associated with psychological disabilities and disclosure requires additional research.

References

Ackerman, G., and McReynolds, C. "Strategies to Promote Successful Employment of People with Psychiatric Disabilities." *Journal of Applied Rehabilitation Counseling*, 2005, 36(4), 35.

Ackerman, R., DiRamio, D., and Mitchell, R. L. "Transitions: Combat Veterans as College Students." In R. Ackerman and D. DiRamio (eds.), *Creating a Veteran-Friendly Campus: Strategies for Transition and Success.* New Directions for Student Services, no. 126. San Francisco: Jossey-Bass, 2009.

American Council on Education. "Serving Those Who Serve: Higher Education and America's Veterans." 2009. http://www.acenet.edu/Content/NavigationMenu/Programs Services/MilitaryPrograms/serving/index.htm.

American Psychiatric Association. *Diagnostic and Statistical Manual of Mental Disorders,* 4th ed., Text Revision. Washington, D.C.: Author, 2000.

Branker, C. "Deserving Design: The New Generation of Student Veterans." *Journal of Postsecondary Education and Disability,* 2009, 22(1), 59–66.

Burk, H., and Degeneffe, C. "A New Disability for Rehabilitation Counselors: Iraq War Veterans with Traumatic Brain Injury and Post Traumatic Stress Disorder." *Journal of Rehabilitation,* 2009, 75(3), 5–14.

Burnett, S. E., and Segoria, J. "Collaboration for Military Transition Students from Combat to College: It Takes a Community." *Journal of Postsecondary Education and Disability,* 2009, 22(1), 53–58.

Church, T. E. "Returning Veterans on Campus with War Related Injuries and the Long Road Back Home." *Journal of Postsecondary Education and Disability,* 2009, 22(1), 43–52.

Cook, B. J., and Kim, Y. *From Soldier to Student: Easing the Transition of Service Members on Campus.* Washington D.C.: American Council on Education, 2009.

DiRamio, D., Ackerman, R., and Mitchell, R. L. "From Combat to Campus: Voices of Student-Veterans." *NASPA Journal,* 2008, 45(1), 73–108.

Drew, D., and others. "Effects of Disability Compensation on Participation in and Outcomes of Vocational Rehabilitation." *Psychiatric Services,* 2001, 52, 1479–1484.

Dutta, A., Schiro-Geist, C., and Kundu, M. M. "Coordination of Postsecondary Transition Services for Students with Disabilities." *Journal of Rehabilitation,* 2009, 75(1), 10–17.

Ford, D., Northrup, P., and Wiley, L. "Connections, Partnerships, Opportunities, and Programs to Enhance Success for Military Students." In R. Ackerman and D. DiRamio (eds.), *Creating a Veteran-Friendly Campus: Strategies for Transition and Success.* New Directions for Student Services, no. 126. San Francisco: Jossey-Bass, 2009.

Frueh, B., Henning, K., Pelligrin, K., and Choboth, K., "Relationship Between Scores on Anger Measures and PTSD Symptomology, Employment and Compensation-Seeking Status in Combat Veterans." *Journal of Clinical Psychology,* 1997, 53(8), 871–878.

Goldberg, M. S. "Death and Injury Rates of U.S. Military Personnel in Iraq." *Military Medicine,* 2010, 175(4), 220–226.

Grossman, P. D. "Forward with a Challenge: Leading Our Campuses Away from the Perfect Storm." *Journal of Postsecondary Education and Disability,* 2009, 22(1), 4–9.

Hall, L. K. "The Importance of Understanding Military Culture." *Social Work in Health Care,* 2011, 50, 4–11.

Holloway, K. M. "Understanding Reentry of the Modern-Day Student-Veteran Through Vietnam Era Theory." *Journal of Student Affairs,* 2009–2010, 18, 11–18.

Human Resources Focus Report: The 2011 ADAAA Regulations: A Guide for Employers, 2011. Old Saybrook, CT: BLR. http://catalog.blr.com/product.cfm/product/30614960.

Institute of Medicine. "Returning Home from Iraq and Afghanistan: Preliminary Assessment of Readjustment Needs of Veterans, Service Members and Their Families." Washington, D.C.: National Academies Press, 2010. www.nap.edu/catalog/12812.html.

Kim, P., and others. "Stigma, Barriers to Care, and Use of Mental Health Services Among Active Duty and National Guard Soldiers After Combat." *Psychiatric Services,* 2010, 61(6), 582–585.

Loughran, D. S., and Klerman, J. A. "Explaining the Increase in Unemployment Compensation for ex-Service Members During the Global War on Terror." Technical Report, RAND, National Defense Research Institute, 2008. www.rand.org/pubs/tech nical_reports/TR588.html.

Madaus, J. W., Miller, W. K., and Vance, M. L. "Veterans with Disabilities in Postsecondary Education." *Journal of Postsecondary Education*, 2009, 22(1), 10–17.

Mueser, K., and others. "Posttraumatic Stress Disorder, Supported Employment, and Outcomes in People with Severe Mental Illness." *CNS Spectrum*, 2004, 9(12), 925.

Pietrzak, R., and others. "Perceived Stigma and Barriers to Mental Health Care Utilization Among OEF-OIF Veterans." *Psychiatric Services*, 2009, 60(8), 1118–1122.

Resnik, L., Plow, M., and Jette, A. "Development of CRIS: Measure of Community Reintegration of Injured Service Members." *Journal of Rehabilitation Research and Development*, 2009, 46(4), 469–480.

Sargeant, W. M., Jr. *Helping Veterans Transition into Academic Life Through the Creation of a University Veteran Support Group: So We Can Better Serve Those Who Served Us.* San Francisco: Jossey-Bass, 2009.

Schlossberg, N. K., Waters, E. B., and Goodman, J. *Counseling Adults in Transition*, 2nd ed. San Francisco: Jossey-Bass, 1995.

Schuman, I., and Hartstein, B. "Final Rule Implementing Employment Provisions of the ADAAA Released." March 25, 2011. www.dcemploymentlawupdate.com/2011/03/ articles/agency-rulemaking/final-rule-implementing-employment-provisions-of-the-adaaa-released/.

Shackleford, A. L. "Documenting the Needs of Student Veterans with Disabilities: Intersection, Roadblocks, Solutions, and Legal Realities." *Journal of Postsecondary Education and Disability*, 2009, 22(1), 36–42.

Street, A., Vogt, D., and Dutra, L. "A New Generation of Women Veterans: Stressors Faced by Women Deployed to Iraq and Afghanistan." *Clinical Psychology Review*, 2009, 29, 685–694.

Sumerlot, J., Green, S. M., and Parker, P. "Student Veteran Organizations." *New Directions for Student Services*, 2009, 126, 71–79.

Summerall, E. L. "Traumatic Brain Injury and PTSD." 2007. www.ptsd.va.gov/profes sional/pages/traumatic-brain-injury-ptsd.asp.

Tanielian, T., and Jaycox, L. (eds.), *Invisible Wounds of War: Psychological and Cognitive Injuries, Their Consequences, and Services to Assist Recovery.* Santa Monica, Calif.: RAND Corporation, 2008.

Tepe, V., and Fendley, M. "Screening and Diagnosis of Military TBI: Review and Analysis." Wright Patterson AFB, Ohio: SURVIAC, 2009.

U.S. Department of Labor. "America's Heroes at Work Supporting the Employment Success of Returning Service Members with TBI & PTSD," n.d. [Brochure]. www.dol.gov/odep/pubs/2010AHW_brochure_508.pdf.

U.S. Department of Veterans Affairs. "Traumatic Brain Injury and PTSD." 2010a. www.ptsd.va.gov/public/pages/traumatic_brain_injury_and_ptsd.asp.

U.S. Department of Veterans Affairs. Veterans Benefits Administration. "Annual Benefits Report: Fiscal Year 2010." 2010b. www.vba.va.gov/REPORTS/abr/2010_abr.pdf.

U.S. Department of Veterans Affairs. Vocational Rehabilitation and Employment Programs. 2011. www.vba.va.gov/bln/vre/index.htm.

U.S. Department of Veterans Affairs. Strategic Plan Refresh: Fiscal Year 2011–2015, n.d. http://va.gov/VA_2011-2015_Strategic_Plan_Refresh_wv.pdf.

Vanderploeg, R. D., and others. "Rehabilitation of Traumatic Brain Injury in Active Duty Military Personnel and Veterans: Defense and Veterans Brain Injury Center Randomized, Controlled Trials of Two Rehabilitation Approaches." *Archives of Physical Medicine and Rehabilitation*, 2008, 89, 2227–2238.

Vasterling, J., and others. "Neuropsychological Outcomes of Army Personnel Following Deployment to the Iraq War." *Journal of American Medical Association,* 2006, 296(5), 519–529.

FARIBA OSTOVARY, ARNP, is a board-certified psychiatric mental health nurse practitioner for the U.S. Department of Veterans Affairs, the Miami VA Health-care System.

JANET DAPPRICH, M.S. Ed., CTRS, specializes in adult education and currently holds the position of veterans health education program manager at the Miami VA Healthcare System, U.S Department of Veterans Affairs.

Since the 1980s, educators in adult basic education and special education have speculated that a substantial if unknown percentage of adults have specific learning disabilities and have sought to identify and address effectively the needs of these learners.

Revisiting Debates on Learning Disabilities in Adult Education

Alisa Belzer, Jovita Ross-Gordon

Since the 1980s, educators in adult basic education and special education have speculated that a substantial if unknown percentage of adults have specific learning disabilities (LDs) (Coles, 1980; Hoy and Gregg, 1984; Ross-Gordon, 1989) and have sought to identify and address effectively the needs of these learners. Although many definitions of specific learning disabilities (SLDs) exist, the National Research Center on Learning Disabilities (2007) offers this definition as a consensus statement from the National Joint Committee on Learning Disabilities:

> The central concept of SLD involves disorders of learning and cognition that are intrinsic to the individual. SLD are specific in the sense that these disorders each significantly affect a relatively narrow range of academic and performance outcomes. SLD may occur in combination with other disabling conditions, but they are not due primarily to other conditions, such as mental retardation, behavioral disturbance, lack of opportunities to learn, or primary sensory deficits. (p. 2)

Two rarely intersecting bodies of historical literature on LDs (Vogel and Reder, 1998) provide the background for this chapter, and two recently produced documents (National Institute for Literacy, 2009; Taymans, 2010) enable us to analyze the ways that LDs among adults are currently understood. However, they reveal a failure to ground research and practice in adult learning theory, a significant gap that may shape the impact of service provision for this population.

NEW DIRECTIONS FOR ADULT AND CONTINUING EDUCATION, no. 132, Winter 2011 © 2011 Wiley Periodicals, Inc.
Published online in Wiley Online Library (wileyonlinelibrary.com) • DOI: 10.1002/ace.433

A Look at the Past

Following the 1975 passage of the Education for All Handicapped Children's Act (Public Law 94-142, most recently amended as the Individuals with Disabilities Education Improvement [IDEA] Act of 2004, Public Law 108-446), practitioners and scholars in the field of LDs became increasingly aware that young people diagnosed with LDs did not outgrow their LDs by the time they left public education. This spawned literature focusing on the characteristics of LDs during adulthood and adult outcomes of individuals with LDs (Bruck, 1985). Similar to research on children with LDs, much of this work focused on topics such as the presumed neurobiological origins of LDs and cognitive functioning (Darden and Morgan, 1996; Riccio and Hynd, 1996). Another strand of work by LD and special education scholars focused on the characteristics of LDs and identification of appropriate accommodations for college-going populations (Aksamit, Morris, and Leuenberger, 1987). In rare instances, scholars focused more broadly on the implications of LDs for adult development and performance of adult life roles (Polloway, Smith, and Patton, 1984).

In the field of adult education, interest in adult LDs emanated largely from literacy providers in adult basic, secondary, and English as a second language programs who wondered why many students did not show typical patterns of progress (Ross and Smith, 1990). Sometimes these educators drew parallels between these students and those diagnosed in public schools as having LDs; others suggested that adult literacy students might learn differently for a number of reasons other than LDs (Ross-Gordon, 1989). Although relatively few adult education students reported previous diagnosis of LDs, adult literacy educators speculated about the prevalence of LD among learners in their programs, with estimates as high as 80 percent (Travis, 1979). While research was lacking to support such estimates (Ross-Gordon, Plotts, Noble, and Wells, 2003), they fueled the demand for greater professional development regarding LD, as reflected in the development of Bridges to Practice, a set of four guidebooks that became the basis for workshops on LDs for literacy practitioners across the country (Bridges to Practice, 1999).

As this brief overview indicates, authors from the fields of adult education and special education have often approached the subject of adult LDs from different perspectives. Those in special education have more commonly emphasized the presumed neurological and cognitive roots of LDs as well as interventions aimed at improving cognitive capacities or assisting adults in developing compensatory strategies. Publications in adult education have generally reflected a practical focus, aimed at screening for LDs and identifying appropriate instructional strategies (Jordan, 2000). Yet with few exceptions (Coles, 1987; Patton and Polloway, 1992; Ross-Gordon, 1996), the literature within both professional fields has shared two common features: greater attention to psychological than sociocultural understandings of LD

New Directions for Adult and Continuing Education • DOI: 10.1002/ace

and limited incorporation of theories of adult learning and development. As the next section of this chapter suggests, key recent documents reporting research on adults with LDs and making recommendations for practice do not signal a shift in this state of affairs.

Current Research and Practice on Adults with Learning Disabilities. Two recently published documents were selected as representative of current adult education research and practice regarding LDs. The first, *Learning to Achieve: A Review of the Research Literature on Serving Adults with Learning Disabilities*, is a review of research (National Institute for Literacy, 2009). *Learning to Achieve: A Professional's Guide to Educating Adults with Learning Disabilities* (Taymans, 2010) is a companion document designed to supplement face-to-face and online LD training developed by the National Institute for Literacy or as a stand-alone practitioner resource.

These two documents are in line with the federal policy goal of making educational practice "research-based" as prescribed by key laws like the No Child Left Behind Act (2002) and the Workforce Investment Act (1998), which provides federal funds for adult and family literacy programs. Documents developed in support of these goals (Kruidenier, 2002; National Institute for Child Health and Development, 2000; Snow and Strucker, 1999) review only experimental or quasi-experimental studies, leaving little or no room to learn from qualitative approaches that help researchers and practitioners understand more about why various practices work, under what circumstances, and for whom. There is an explicit assumption that "best practices" can be identified and applied in schools and programs unproblematically with a high level of generalizability.

Similarly, the *Learning to Achieve* review was conducted to "provide a specific, coherent evidence base" (National Institute for Literacy, 2009, p. 5) for the instruction of adults with LDs. The author of the report's introduction suggests that such a document can counteract the tendency in the field to base instruction on practices that may be "popular but [are] unproven or even discredited. Armed with such information, service providers can make educated choices about the interventions they offer" (p. 9). Like similar documents, this one implies that if only the field would follow the research, it could more successfully serve the needs of the learner.

The document reviews the literature on defining and identifying what constitutes an LD, identification of adults with LDs, issues specific to identification of LDs for English-language learners, assessment and instructional accommodations, instructional strategies, transitions to beyond school for adults with LDs, and the impact of LDs in adulthood. Although chapter authors did not always state selection criteria for the research reviewed, they included only what many of them called "empirical" studies using experimental or quasi-experimental designs. There was virtually no reference to any qualitative research. Unfortunately, few definitive findings emerged from this review due largely to an oft-stated paucity of research specific to the questions posed by chapter authors. The topics not illuminated by this comprehensive review include a clear definition of LD in adulthood, a prescriptive strategy for identifying LD for native and nonnative speakers of English, whether readers with LDs need different instructional strategies from other low-achieving readers, the effectiveness of most instructional and testing accommodations and many instructional interventions, and what supports are needed for adults with LDs to make transition successfully into adulthood. What can be said with some certainty is that adults with LDs can benefit from extended instructional and assessment time and explicit and intensive instruction with extensive practice and elaborated feedback. The report concludes by asserting that the research base is not adequate to guide practice, and, furthermore, it is not informed by "a conceptual model to investigate adult issues. . . . It is lacking the context of adult development and its many phases" (National Institute for Literacy, 2009, p. 245).

The assertion made at the end of the research review that, when it comes to serving adults with LDs, one size cannot fit all, did not preclude the development of a *Professional's Guide* to practice. Although the author claims that the research review is its foundation, much of the document skirts the lack of research available on adults with LDs by focusing either on topics not covered by the literature review (the importance of learners exercising self-determination) or providing instructional strategies not specific to adults (e.g., explicit instruction, reading).

These documents seem to reflect the medical/scientific understanding of LDs, which suggests that when adequate scientific research is carried out and analyzed, we can meet the needs of adult learners effectively. However, not only does the *Professional's Guide* fail to provide an adequate research-based instructional approach, it fails to account for what we understand about the nature of adult learning, adult development, and the impact of culture on the way adults, including those with LDs, experience learning and related implications for practice. In the next section, we use these three lenses to analyze and critique these documents as a way to gain a broader perspective on serving adults with LDs.

Adult Learning Theories Lens

A holistic framework for understanding adult learning articulated by Boucouvalas and Lawrence (2010) suggests that adult learners participate in multiple contexts and are constituted of multiple identities, each with distinctive practices, values, and beliefs. This means that reducing any adult to one dimension, such as his or her LD, cannot adequately inform practice. Thus, narrowly proscribed research reviews cannot address the complexity of responding to adults with LDs. Practice should not simply be driven by what we know about cognitive domains or testable interventions but also by what we know about somatic and affective learning as well as spiritual, artistic, and transpersonal ways of knowing (Boucouvalas and Lawrence,

2010). A holistic view of adult learners tends to affirm one of the least helpful but most important conclusions of the *Learning to Achieve* literature
review: One size cannot fit all.

Experiential adult learning approaches encourage learners to construct
new knowledge based on individual and collaborative reflection on prior
and current experiences as well as classroom-based, constructed experiences
(Tennant and Pogson, 1995). For example, reflection on experiences of
being diagnosed and learning with a disability could be utilized to develop
more sophisticated and complex understandings of obstacles and needed
supports for learning as well as involving the learner in collaboratively craft-
ing effective strategies for learning. Andragogy, the oft-cited principles of
adult learning articulated by Knowles (Knowles, Holton, and Swanson,
1998), and the tenets of self-directed learning (Tough, 1971) highlight the
importance of learners playing an active role in planning, designing, and
guiding their own instruction. Learners themselves are uniquely situated to
play a key role in their own learning (Brookfield, 1991). Integrating explicit
vocabulary instruction described in the *Professional's Guide* (Taymans, 2010)
with texts that are part of learners' everyday experiences or that address
learners' interests and goals is a far more "adult" approach to reading than
is evidenced in the *Guide*.

Subscribing to the more medicalized view of adults with disabilities
suggested by the literature review and *Professional's Guide* makes it almost
natural for practitioners to fall into the role of caretakers and decision mak-
ers and jettison the principles of adult learning. Yet there is no evidence to
suggest that adult learners with LDs are any less able to take up adult roles
than other learners. Adult learners with LDs, given "appropriate amounts
of structure and support" (Ross-Gordon, 1998), can be involved in every
step of the process should they choose to.

Adult Development Lens

Although marginally reflected in the *Learning to Achieve* documents and
rarely reflected in earlier literature (Gerber and Reiff, 1994; Polloway, Smith,
and Patton, 1984), models of adult development suggest ways to improve
educational programs and practices directed toward this learner population.
The most frequently referenced models of adult development are stage models, based on the premise that adults move through sequential and progres-
sive stages toward more mature levels of development. Stage models have
focused on cognitive development (Baseeches, 1985), moral development
(Kohlberg, 1981), and developing levels of consciousness (Kegan, 1994).
These models share a view of the maturing adult as increasingly, although not
universally, moving from dualistic thinking to increasingly multiplistic thinking in which the merits of competing knowledge claims are recognized and
decisions are based on complex personal, relational, and contextual factors.

New Directions for Adult and Continuing Education • DOI: 10.1002/ace

As the title of Robert Kegan's book—*In Over Our Heads: The Mental Demands of Modern Life*—suggests, like other adults, those with LDs often find themselves "in over their heads" as they attempt to navigate and balance competing demands of adult life. Educators aware of these developmental models may be better prepared to design educational programs that assist adults in developing the critical and dialectical thinking needed to successfully navigate adult roles, including those of parent, partner, and worker. For instance, while chapters in the *Learning to Achieve* documents discuss the importance of self-determination and describe how to help adults with LDs in developing skills for self-disclosure and self-advocacy, neither volume treats in any substantive way the kinds of complex decision making that adults likely will go through in making cost-benefit decisions about when, how, and with whom to engage in self-disclosure regarding the existence of their invisible disability.

Another set of frameworks for adult development emphasizes these life roles themselves (Hughes and Graham, 1990) and the life events and transitions that adults experience (Merriam, 2005). Life events and transitions often challenge adults' existing ways of thinking and behaving, and in so doing they may serve as a catalyst for transformational learning (Mezirow and associates, 1990). As Merriam (2005) has noted, the potential for learning and development from a life event is often linked to the timing of the life event. Life events occurring at unpredicted times may create a sense of disequilibrium and hence an opportunity to change. So may the nonoccurrence of expected events, as may happen when an adult with LDs is not able to establish an independent residence away from parents due to difficulties finding adequate employment. Our examination of the *Professional's Guide* indicates that relatively little consideration is given to adults' varied life roles. Incorporating adult tasks and roles into learning activities through recognition of life event and transition models could lead to lessons that are more meaningful to adults with LDs.

Sociocultural Lens

The two documents described earlier construct images of LD as uncontested and of adults with LD as culturally neutral. In these two documents, LD is a brain-based dysfunction, and best practices derived from experimental research can be prescribed equally effectively for every learner with the same cognitive issues. It seems implied that race, class, and gender play no role in what constitutes appropriate practice. This implication can negatively influence LD identification, assessment, application of appropriate practice, and learner engagement.

In contrast, Ross-Gordon (1996) suggests that LD is an educational category that "has been socially constructed, defined, and utilized" (p. 89), implying the need for a more varied instructional response. Because students

New Directions for Adult and Continuing Education • DOI: 10.1002/ace

with LDs may be those whom teachers feel inadequately prepared to help, the term can be an artifact of the demands and expectations of schooling rather than designating a difficulty that necessarily manifests itself universally in all contexts (Sleeter as cited in Ross-Gordon, 1996). Coles (1987, as cited in Ross-Gordon, 1996) asserts that a relatively small number of people who are diagnosed as having LDs have an actual neurological dysfunction; others may simply vary from social constructions of "normal." Although Coles's argument has been critiqued, he has helped the field consider the ways in which context shapes understanding of LDs (Ross-Gordon, 1996).

Making race, class, and gender invisible in LD research and practice creates a problem of under- and overidentifying LDs. Assessment and testing can be rendered inaccurate by inherent bias (Ross-Gordon, 1998) and inability to adequately account for second-language learners (National Institute for Literacy, 2009). Additionally, there is little acknowledgment of the ways in which culture and gender may impact access to services or ability to fully participate, although they may play a role in significantly slowing progress for reasons that have little to do with disability.

At least as relevant is the deleterious effect on learners and learning of making culture invisible. When learning is construed as "neutral," it generally reifies mainstream, dominant values (Guy, 1999). Guy (1999) suggests that adult education is an arena in which these patterns can and should be interrupted by reevaluating "educational norms, processes, and goals" (p. 12). Although discussing race, the assertions of Isaac, Merriweather, and Rogers (2010) can be generalized to all marginalized learners when they suggest that failure to attend to the "pivotal" role race plays in teaching and learning can impact "access to learning, quality of instruction, feelings of being unwelcomed, and the ability to persist" (p. 363).

Perspectives on LDs that do not explicitly acknowledge that race, class, and gender shape teaching and learning deny important dimensions of the educational dynamic. Guy (1999) asserts that instructional practices should be culturally compatible and include practices that maximize participation, choice, and decision making in appropriate ways for all students, including those with LDs. Given the challenges adults with LDs often face in formal educational settings, doing so may be even more important for them than for other students.

Conclusion

Experimental studies and meta-analyses like those reported in *Learning to Achieve* can play a role in informing instruction and are important for addressing the current calls for research-based practice. However, the field need not slavishly attend only to one type of empirical method. Rather, we need to seek an integration of diverse research methods with adult learning

New Directions for Adult and Continuing Education • DOI: 10.1002/ace

theory and consideration of learner context. When the findings of experimental studies demonstrate effective instructional strategies, we should use them. Using experimental studies and meta-analyses should not be to the exclusion of building on what we know qualitatively about adult learners and learning. These may be concepts and practices that defy experimental study because of the unique and multitudinous differences in adults and the varied contexts and purposes for learning. We need to resist a false division between a cognitive/physiological stance on disability and a socially constructed understanding of adults who have difficulty learning if we are to truly meet the needs of adult learners with LDs.

References

Aksamit, D., Morris, M., and Leuenberger, L. "Preparation of Student Services Professionals and Faculty for Serving Learning-Disabled College Students." *Journal of College Student Personnel*, 1987, 28(1), 53–59.

Basseches, M. *Dialectical Thinking and Adult Development*. Norwood, N.J.: Albex, 1985.

Boucouvalis, M., and Lawrence, R. L. "Adult Learning." In C. E. Kasworm, A. D. Rose, and J. M. Ross-Gordon (eds.), *Handbook of Adult and Continuing Education*. Thousand Oaks, Calif.: Sage, 2010.

Bridges to Practice. *A Research-Based Guide for Literacy Practitioners Serving Adults with Learning Disabilities*. Washington, D.C.: Academy for Educational Development. (ED 426 237.)

Brookfield, S. *Understanding and Facilitating Adult Learning*. San Francisco: Jossey-Bass, 1991.

Bruck, M. "The Adult Functioning of Children with Specific Learning Disabilities: A Follow-Up Study. In I. Seigel (ed.), *Advances in Applied Developmental Psychology*, vol. 1. Norwood, N.J.: Albex, 1985.

Coles, G. S. "Can ABE Students Be Identified as Learning Disabled?" *Adult Literacy and Basic Education*, 1980, 4(3), 170–181.

Coles, G. S. *The Learning Mystique: A Critical Look at Learning Disabilities*. New York: Pantheon, 1987.

Darden, C. A., and Morgan, A. W. "Cognitive Functioning Profiles of the Adult Population with Learning Disabilities." In N. Gregg, C. Hoy, and A. F. Gay (eds.), *Adults with Learning Disabilities*. New York: Guilford Press, 1996.

Education for All Handicapped Children's Act of 1975, Public Law 94-142, U.S. Code 20, § 1400.

Gerber, P. J., and Rieff, H. B. (eds.), *Learning Disabilities in Adulthood: Persisting Problems and Evolving Issues*. Stoneham, Mass.: Butterworth-Heinemann, 1994.

Guy, T. C. *Culture as Context for Adult Education: The Need for Culturally Relevant Adult Education*. New Directions for Adult and Continuing Education, no. 82. San Francisco: Jossey-Bass, 1999.

Hoy, C. A., and Gregg K. N. *Description and Definition of Learning Disabilities. Academic Assessment and Remediation of Adults with Learning Disabilities: A Resource Series for Adult Basic Education Teachers*, Athens, Ga.: Clarke County Board of Education, 1984. (ERIC Document No. 284 354.)

Hughes, J. A., and Graham, S. W. "Adult Life Roles: A New Approach to Adult Development." *Journal of Continuing Higher Education*, 1990, 38(2), 2–8.

Individuals with Disabilities Education Improvement Act of 2004 (IDEA), Public Law 108-446, U.S. Code 20, § 1400.

Isaac, E. P., Merriweather, L. R., and Rogers, E. E. "Chasing the American Dream: Race and Adult and Continuing Education." In C. E. Kasworm, A. D. Rose, and J. M. Ross-Gordon (eds.), *Handbook of Adult and Continuing Education, 2010 Edition*. Thousand Oaks, Calif.: Sage, 2010.

Jordan, D. R. *Teaching Adults with Learning Disabilities*. Malabar, Fla.: Krieger Publishing, 1996.

Kegan, R. *In Over Our Heads: The Mental Demands of Modern Life*. Cambridge, Mass.: Harvard University Press. 1994.

Knowles, M. S., Holton, E. F., and Swanson, R. A. *The Adult Learner*. Woburn, Mass.: Butterworth-Heinemann, 1998.

Kohlberg, L. *The Philosophy of Moral Development: Moral Stages and the Idea of Justice*. New York: Harper & Row, 1981.

Kruidenier, J. *Research-Based Principles of Adult Basic Education Reading Instruction*. Portsmouth, N.H.: RMC Research, 2002.

Merriam, S. B. "How Adult Life Transitions Foster Learning and Development." In M. A. Wolf (ed.), *Adulthood: New Terrain*. New Directions for Adult and Continuing Education, no. 108. San Francisco: Jossey-Bass, 2005.

Mezirow, J., and Associates. *Fostering Critical Reflection in Adulthood: A Guide to Transformative Learning*. San Francisco: Jossey-Bass, 1990.

National Institute for Child Health and Development. Report of the National Reading Panel: Teaching Children to Read: An Evidence-Based Assessment of the Scientific Research Literature on Reading and Its Implication for Reading Instruction, Washington, D.C.: Author, 2000. NIH Pub. No. 00-4769.

National Institute for Literacy. *Learning to Achieve: A Review of the Research Literature on Serving Adults with Learning Disabilities*. Washington, D.C.: Author 2009.

National Research Center on Learning Disabilities. "SLD Identification Overview: General Information and Tools to Get Started." Winter 2007. www.nrcld.org/resource_kit/tools/SLDOverview2007.pdf.

No Child Left Behind Act of 2001, Public Law 107-110, U.S. Code 20, § 6301.

Patton, J. R., and Polloway, E. A. "Learning Disabilities: The Challenges of Adulthood." *Journal of Learning Disabilities*, 1992, *25*, 410–415.

Polloway, E. A., Smith, J. D., and Patton, J. R. "Learning Disabilities: An Adult Development Perspective." *Learning Disabilities Quarterly*, 1984, *7*, 179–186.

Riccio, C. A., and Hynd, G. W. "Neurobiological Research Specific to the Adult Population with Learning Disabilities," In N. Gregg, C. Hoy, and A. F. Gay (eds.), *Adults with Learning Disabilities*. New York: Guilford Press, 1996.

Ross, J. M., and Smith, J. O. "Adult Basic Educators' Perceptions of Learning Disabilities." *Journal of Reading*, 1990, *33*(5), 340–347.

Ross-Gordon, J. M. "Adults with Learning Disabilities: An Overview for the Adult Educator." ERIC Information Paper, 1989. (ERIC Document No. 337.)

Ross-Gordon, J. M. "Literacy Education for Adults with Learning Disabilities: Perspectives from the Adult Education Side of the Mirror." In S. A. Vogel and S. Reder (eds.), *Learning Disabilities, Literacy, and Adult Education*. Baltimore, Md.: Paul H. Brookes Publishing, 1998.

Ross-Gordon, J. M. "Sociocultural Issues Affecting the Identification and Service Delivery Models for Adults with Learning Disabilities." In N. Gregg, C. Hoy and A. F. Gay (eds.), *Adults with Learning Disabilities*. New York: Guilford Press, 1996.

Ross-Gordon, J. M., Plotts, C., Noble, J., and Wells, R. "Assessment of Adult Learning Disabilities: Multiple Perspectives." *Adult Basic Education: An Interdisciplinary Journal for Adult Literacy Educator*, 2003, *13*(3), 131–145.

Snow, C., and Strucker, J. "Lessons from Preventing Reading Difficulties in Young Children for Adult Learning and Literacy." In J. Coming, B. Garner and C. Smith (eds.), *Review of Adult Learning and Literacy*. Boston: NCSALL, 1999.

Taymans, J. M. *Learning to Achieve: A Professional's Guide to Educating Adults with Learning Disabilities*. Washington, D.C.: National Institute for Literacy, 2010.

Tennant, M., and Pogson, P. *Learning and Change in the Adult Years*. San Francisco: Jossey-Bass, 1995.

Tough, A. *The Adult's Learning Projects: A Fresh Approach to Theory and Practice in Adult Learning*. Toronto: Ontario Institute for Studies in Education, 1971.

Travis, G. Y. "An Adult Educator Views Learning Disabilities." *Adult Literacy and Basic Education*, 1979, 3, 85–92.

Vogel, S. A., and Reder S. (eds.), *Learning Disabilities, Literacy, and Adult Education*. Baltimore, Md.: Paul H. Brookes Publishing, 1998.

Workforce Investment Act of 1998, Public Law 105-220, U.S. Code 29, § 2940.

ALISA BELZER is an associate professor in the Department of Learning and Teaching at Rutgers University, the State University of New Jersey.

JOVITA ROSS-GORDON is director of Education Ph.D. Programs in the Counseling, Leadership, Adult Education, and School Psychology Department at Texas State University—San Marcos.

9

As a result of the amendments to the Americans with Disabilities Act and its parallel revisions to Section 504 of the Rehabilitation Act of 1973, plaintiffs are more likely to clear the disability hurdle; therefore, we can expect to see much more litigation in the future focused on complex ADA issues regarding reasonable accommodations and undue hardship.

Americans with Disabilities Act as Amended: Principles and Practice

Lorenzo Bowman

The purpose of this chapter is to provide an overview of the Americans with Disabilities Act (ADA) and the 2008 amendments to the act (ADAAA) as well as Section 504 of the Rehabilitation Act of 1973. The chapter describes the major sections of the ADA, addresses the changes brought about to the ADA and Section 504 as a result of the ADAAA, reviews the outcome of initial court cases and settlement agreements filed under the ADAAA, and concludes with a discussion of implications for recruiters, hiring managers, department heads, and adult and higher education.

In 1990, the ADA, comprised of three titles, was passed into law by Congress. This long-awaited piece of federal legislation was expected to protect individuals with disabilities from discrimination in employment opportunities and ensure access to various social institutions. ADA Title I is the employment title. It requires that employers not discriminate against individuals who, with reasonable accommodations, can perform the essential functions of the job. ADA Title II covers nearly any program or activity conducted by a public entity ranging from adult and higher education to prisons to public healthcare. This title broadens the coverage already existing under Section 504 of the Rehabilitation Act of 1973. Section 504 prohibits organizations receiving federal financial assistance from discriminating on the basis of disability. Because most branches of state or local government receive federal financial assistance, ADA Title II and Section 504 are often coextensive. The only activity funded by state or local governments that ADA Title II and Section 504 do not typically regulate is primary and secondary education, because that area is primarily regulated by the Individuals with Disabilities Education Act (IDEA). The IDEA allows students to

NEW DIRECTIONS FOR ADULT AND CONTINUING EDUCATION, no. 132, Winter 2011 © 2011 Wiley Periodicals, Inc.
Published online in Wiley Online Library (wileyonlinelibrary.com) • DOI: 10.1002/ace.434

receive disability services until they graduate high school or, as older high school students, up through age twenty-one. Once a student enters college, the ADA, the ADAAA, and Section 504 provide protection from disability discrimination (National Center for Learning Disabilities, 2011). Since this chapter focuses on the impact of the ADA amendment on adult and higher education and employment, the IDEA will not be addressed. Last, Title III of the ADA protects individuals with disabilities from discrimination and requires accessibility at public places, such as government, food, lodging, and healthcare establishments; places that enhance the quality of life, such as hotels, restaurants; and places for entertainment and recreation (Colker, 2001).

After passage of the 1990 Act, it became evident that most of the decisions handed down by the federal courts were prodefendant. In three decisions issued by the United States Supreme Court in 1999 (*Albertsons, Inc. v. Kirkingburg*, 1999; *Murphy v. United Parcel Service*, 1999; *Sutton et al. v. United Air Lines*, 1999) and followed by a decision in 2002 (*Toyota Motor Manufacturing, Kentucky, Inc. v. Williams*), the Supreme Court severely narrowed the playing field for disability discrimination plaintiffs. These decisions required the lower courts to strictly apply a "demanding standard" when trying to determine whether a plaintiff was considered disabled to advance an ADA lawsuit. The court also overturned Equal Employment Opportunity Commission (EEOC) regulations that required employers to determine whether an employee was disabled without mitigating measures. This meant that where corrective treatment or corrective devices could be used to control or ameliorate the condition, then that person was not deemed to be disabled under the Act as a result of the court's limiting rulings. Some courts even found that individuals with serious conditions such as diabetes and cancer were not covered by the ADA's protections against discrimination (U.S. Equal Employment Opportunity Commission, 2010a, b).

However, education cases under Section 504 were more successful for plaintiffs than the employment cases under ADA or Section 504. The low success rate for employment cases did appear to impact plaintiffs' success rate in Section 504 cases involving education discrimination. During the past decade, there has been a clear trend toward less successful outcomes for plaintiffs in employment cases (Colker, 2001).

Disability advocates lobbied Congress for change over the course of more than eight years beginning in 2000. The political forces in support of change finally became strong enough to reform the ADA, and the ADAAA went into effect on January 1, 2009.

What Changed?

The ADAAA requires that almost all human resource professionals, managers, business owners, and educational institutions of higher learning adopt or revise existing policies and procedures when dealing with accommodation requests under the ADA. Under the amended ADA, the threshold issue of whether an individual has a disability within the meaning of the ADA will no longer be the focus of most litigation. Instead, the focus of future litigation under the amended Act likely will be on the individual's ability to perform the essential functions of a job and whether the employer or institution of higher learning met its obligations to engage in the interactive process and provide a reasonable accommodation. Additionally, legal observers expect that there will be an increase in "regarded as" litigation. The "regarded as" clause protects employees where the employer assumes or perceives the employee to have a disability and renders an adverse employment action based on the employer's perception of impairment (Business and Legal Resources, 2011).

The six most significant changes brought about by the passage of the ADAAA are:

1. *The pool of individuals considered disabled is now larger.* However, the definition of "disability" remains the same: A physical or mental impairment that substantially limits one or more major life activities, a record of such an impairment, or being regarded as having such an impairment. The ADAAA makes it clear who Congress intends to meet the definition of disabled (Association on Higher Education and Disability, n.d. a). The revised Act instructs courts and employers to embrace a broad standard when attempting to determine whether an individual is "disabled" within the meaning of the Act. The Act requires that the courts provide protection for plaintiffs "to the maximum extent permitted" by the statute.

2. *Mitigating measures are to be ignored.* Before the ADAAA, several Supreme Court decisions established that the principle of whether an individual has a disability under the ADA must take into account the effects, both positive and negative, of any "mitigating" or "corrective treatment" used by the individual. The ADAAA requires that this decision now be made without regard to the impact of the "corrective treatment" or "mitigating measure." For example, schools can no longer consider the effect of medication on students with attention deficit/hyperactivity disorder (AD/HD), asthma, or diabetes, just to name a few. The ADAAA provides an expansive list of "mitigating measures," including medication, medical supplies, low-vision devices (except eyeglasses or contact lenses), hearing aids, and cochlear implants. Individuals with human immunodeficiency virus are all covered under the Act even if their drug cocktails may have rendered the virus virtually undetectable (Webber, 2011). Where previously a diabetic or someone with AD/HD whose condition was controlled by medication was probably not disabled in light of the prevailing court decisions, now the ADAAA makes it clear that such individuals are probably covered by the Act (Zappe, 2008). We will have to wait for

New Directions for Adult and Continuing Education • DOI: 10.1002/ace

cases to make their way through the legal system before we can know for sure how courts will interpret the revisions. This amendment reverses prior Supreme Court decisions (*Toyota Motor Manufacturing, Kentucky, Inc. v. Williams*, 2002) in which the court used a narrow interpretation of the definition of "disability."

3. *The list of what constitutes a "major life activity" has significantly expanded.* Prior to the revision, the ADA was silent on what constituted a "major life activity." The courts typically defined such activities through lists. "Major life activities" are those areas of life that needed to be adversely impacted in order for someone to have a disability within the meaning of the ADA. The EEOC proposed a broad list of activities under the old Act; however, many courts rejected this list. The revisions include a thorough and exhaustive list of activities, which include caring for oneself, performing manual tasks, eating, sleeping, concentrating, thinking, communicating, walking, and working (Fisher & Phillips LLP, 2008; Kaloi, n.d.). This new expansive list almost ensures that anyone who wants to will now be able to file a claim under the ADA.

4. *The "regarded as" prong is more broadly read.* The ADA has always provided protection to those who were "regarded" as having a disability. However, under the old Act, the plaintiff had to prove that the employer regarded the person as being substantially limited in a major life activity, a difficult standard to meet. Under the revised Act, a plaintiff will need only to show that the employer perceived the plaintiff as having a mental or physical impairment. Nevertheless, those employees with "transitory" and "minor" impairments are not covered under the revised "regarded as" prong. A transitory impairment is defined as an impairment lasting six months or less. Also, "regarded as" disabled employees are entitled to reasonable accommodation under the ADA.

5. *The EEOC is permitted to regulate the ADA and define "substantial limitation."* This mandate to the EEOC is noteworthy because the U.S. Supreme Court had expressly called into question the EEOC's authority to issue binding regulations and other interpretative guidance under the old Act. The revised Act gives the EEOC the authority to interpret and enforce the Act. The revised Act specifically requests that the EEOC provide a regulatory definition for the term "substantially limits" that lowers the standard to a level consistent with congressional intent. This change in the Act will mean that the EEOC will issue new regulations expanding the "substantially limits" definition with a pro-employee and expansive bent. The ADAAA makes it clear that the new standard will be less stringent and will not require an impairment to be as serious as under the interpretations of ADA prior to the passage of the amendments.

6. *Other additions and amendments to the Act.* Impairments that are "episodic or in remission" can still be considered to be disabling if they

substantially limit major life activity when active. The revised Act makes an attempt to conform to Title VII of the 1964 Civil Rights Act and other antidiscrimination statutes by changing the past technical language to clearly demonstrate that a plaintiff can prevail in court by showing discrimination "because of" the protected disability. Last, the revised Act prohibits "reverse discrimination" claims. Those not covered under the ADA cannot sue claiming that they were impermissibly discriminated against in favor of someone with a disability.

The ADAAA does not make significant changes to an employer's or an educational institution's obligations of nondiscrimination or reasonable accommodation; it simply dramatically expands the pool of individuals who are now considered to be disabled. Also, the ADAAA keeps the existing exclusions for sex-based conditions and psychological-criminal conditions in place. This means that transvestism and gender-identity disorder are still not covered by the act; nor are kleptomania and pyromania (Culotta, 2010). Nevertheless, these revisions will mean that employers can no longer count on being able to have a disability claim dismissed prior to court. Employers and institutions of higher learning should take ADA claims much more seriously in the future. The revisions have put the ADA on par with other discrimination claims (gender, race, religion, age, etc.). It is no longer difficult for plaintiffs to prove that they have a right to bring a claim under the ADA.

Testing the Waters: The First Court Cases Under the ADAAA

In August 2010, the United States District Court for the Northern District of Indiana (Fort Wayne Division) heard the case of *Hoffman v. Carefirst of Fort Wayne, Inc., d/b/a Advanced Healthcare*. The employee plaintiff in this case was diagnosed with renal cancer. After taking time off, the employee returned to work. One year later, while the cancer was in remission, the employee requested that his work schedule be adjusted as an accommodation. The company mandated overtime for all employees. The company agreed to limit Hoffman's hours to 40 hours per week but required him to work at an office location that added two to three hours of travel per day. Hoffman sued for disability discrimination under the ADA, as amended by the ADAAA, alleging that his company terminated him in violation of the ADA without offering a reasonable accommodation. The company argued that Hoffman did not have a disability under the Act—especially since his cancer was in remission. The company argued that there was no substantial limitation of a major life activity. Relying on the ADAAA, the federal district court rejected the company's argument that Hoffman's cancer, which was in remission, did not constitute a disability because there was no substantial limitation on a major life activity at the time of his job reassignment. According to the *Hoffman* court, the ADAAA makes it clear that an impairment that is episodic or in remission is a disability if it would substantially limit a major life activity when active. The court concluded that given these revised guidelines under the ADAAA, Hoffman's condition constituted a disability (Cino, 2010).

In *Grizzell v. Cyber City Teleservices Marketing, Inc.* (2010), an employee was sent to the Philippines for job training, where he witnessed the death of a young girl. The experience traumatized the plaintiff. The plaintiff had previously been diagnosed with posttraumatic stress disorder (PTSD). The employee informed the employer that he might need treatment for PTSD. The employer refused the request. A few weeks later, the employee was fired. The employee sued under the ADAAA. The employer filed a motion with the court to dismiss the lawsuit; the court refused to dismiss and noted that PTSD is a disability under the ADAAA and as such the case should go to trial (McClure, 2010).

In *Jenkins v. National Board of Medical Examiners* (2009), Jenkins, a medical student, had been diagnosed with a reading disorder at a young age. Nevertheless, Jenkins successfully completed high school, college, and had reached his third year of medical school before his reading disorder presented an insurmountable challenge. The National Board of Medical Examiners refused to provide Jenkins with additional time on an upcoming test. Jenkins sued for injunctive relief. At trial, the court applied the old, restrictive standard for determining disability and found that Jenkins was not disabled within the meaning of the ADA. Jenkins appealed to the Sixth Circuit Court of Appeals. The Sixth Circuit court applied the ADAAA new standards and found that Jenkins was disabled (U.S. Equal Employment Opportunity Commission, 2010a, b).

The National Federation of the Blind filed suit against the Law School Admissions Council arguing that the council's Web site was not fully accessible to blind students. The Admissions Council entered into a settlement agreement with National Federation of the Blind to make its Web site fully accessible to blind students by making the Web site meet the nonvisual requirements of Web Content Accessibility Guidelines (WCAG) 2.0, level AA, so that blind guests using screen-reader software could access the Web site (Catholic University of America, Office of General Counsel, 2011). WCAG are a set of guidelines on making Web content accessible for disabled users. The current version is 2.0; there are three priority levels, Levels A, AA, and AAA. At the middle level (AA), some disabled groups will find it difficult to access the Web content, but most will not (W3C, 2008).

In every ADAAA case the courts have ruled on to date, the plaintiff has been found to have been disabled within the meaning of the ADAAA. This is a major shift in outcomes for employers. Employers and educational institutions should now expect that plaintiffs will be able to easily prove the existence of a disability under the ADAAA. In addition, the EEOC's initial actions under the ADAAA seem to indicate that the agency has renewed its commitment to end disability discrimination. In the short time that the ADAAA has been the law, the agency has vigorously enforced the broader and simplified definition of disability set forth in the ADAAA. For example, the agency charged Eckerd Corporation, a nationwide drug store doing business as Rite Aid in the Northern District of Georgia, with refusing to provide a reasonable accommodation. An employee, who was a cashier, asked for a stool to sit on because of her arthritic knees. The employee was allowed to use the stool for seven years until a new district manager decided to take it away. This action was deemed discriminatory.

The EEOC alleged in charges against Fisher, Collins & Carter, a surveying company, that the company terminated two employees because they had diabetes and hypertension. The company asked the plaintiffs and other employees to complete a questionnaire regarding their health conditions and medications. The suit alleges that despite the employees' many years of successful job performance with the company, they were unlawfully selected for a reduction in force on the bases of their disabilities (U.S. Equal Employment Opportunity Commission, 2010). The EEOC charged IPC Print Services with violation of the ADAAA when the company refused to allow an employee to work part time while being treated for cancer; instead the company fired the employee (U.S. Equal Employment Opportunity Commission, 2010a, b). The EEOC's actions in each of the cases illustrate that the agency is vigorously enforcing the new ADAAA. According to David Lopez, general counsel with the EEOC, Congress has made it very clear that the scope of the ADAAA is broad: Employees with serious medical conditions, such as cancer, diabetes, and severe arthritis, are disabled under the Act. As such they must be evaluated according to their qualifications, not their disabilities (U.S. Equal Employment Opportunity Commission, 2010a, b). Where a reasonable accommodation will enable an employee with a disability to perform the essential functions of a job, an employer must provide it.

Section 504 of the Rehabilitation Act and the ADAAA

Section 504 of the Rehabilitation Act of 1973 applies to all programs and activities that receive federal financial assistance. This includes public schools, colleges and universities as well as certain employers, state and local government programs, and places of public accommodation (e.g., public libraries). Both the ADA and Section 504 are civil rights laws that protect individuals with disabilities from discrimination.

The ADAAA includes a "conforming amendment" to Section 504 of the Rehabilitation Act. This means that the newly expanded coverage under ADAAA also applies to Section 504. This is no surprise since historically the ADA and Section 504 have been interpreted in parallel. Since the ADAAA significantly increases the number of people considered disabled, there are now more students considered to be disabled. It is now much easier for students to file claims of disability without having to worry about whether they meet the legal definition of disabled or not (Kaloi and Stanberry, 2009).

Implications for Recruiters, Hiring Managers, Department Heads, and Adult Educators

While the impact of the ADAAA on hiring managers and recruiters is expected to be somewhat subtle, there are some distinctive changes that they will have to make in their practices. These changes include:

- *Write clear job descriptions.* It is now of critical importance that job descriptions take all of the requirements of a job into account. Including physical weight-lifting requirements, as has historically been the case, is not enough. Job descriptions need to also address mental and emotional requirements (Zappe, 2008).
- *Accommodations can now be requested during the interview process.* Employment kiosks historically used during job fairs and other public venues may have to be modified or alternatives offered to accommodate candidates who request accommodations.
- *The old rules regarding "illegal" questions still apply.* For example, employers should not ask someone whether she has a disability. Similarly, employers cannot ask whether an employee has ever received worker's compensation. Nevertheless, employers have to be even more vigilant during the interview process and be careful not to venture into forbidden territory because under the ADAAA more candidates can be considered disabled. Interviewers have to ensure that every question that is asked and every requirement in the job description is directly related to business necessity (Zappe, 2008). How a question is presented to an applicant can give rise to a claim of discrimination. Employers should restrict inquiries regarding an employee's ability to perform something simple, such as "Are you able to perform all of the essential functions in the job description?" (Sample, 2007, p. 38).
- *Managers, department heads, and adult educators must be trained to be proactive about accommodations.* Now that the pool of potential disabled employees has significantly widened, the danger of "failure to accommodate" lawsuits has increased. Managers, department heads, and adult educators should never immediately refuse a request to accommodate or fail to seriously engage in the necessary interactive process to arrive at a "reasonable accommodation." Once a student provides evidence of a disability, educational institutions are responsible for providing reasonable accommodations or modifications that

will allow the student to participate in the program (Rocco and Fornes, 2010).

- Adult educators, trainers, and other human resource and organizational development professionals must be aware of which laws they operate under in delivering their professional services so that they will know how to respond. Programs that provide services to adults, such as adult basic education classes, and that are funded by federal sources are subject to Section 504 of the Rehabilitation Act of 1973, the ADA, and the ADAAA. Trainers must assess the delivery tools used in working with adults and be prepared to offer accommodations upon request. The Association on Higher Education and Disability (n.d. b) has lists and information on accommodations for different impairments.

Implications for Adult and Higher Education

If an educational institution receives federal funding, it is covered by Section 504 of the Rehabilitation Act of 1973; therefore, once students present evidence of a disability, institutions must undertake efforts to make reasonable accommodations that not only include extra time on texts and exams, but also books and other instructional aids in alternative formats as well as interpreters for lectures. The key is communication. The best course of action is for instructors and advisors to meet with the student once a disability has been documented and discuss the appropriate accommodations prior to the start of the course (Rocco and Fornes, 2010).

Prior to the passage of the ADAAA and its resultant impact on Section 504 of the Rehabilitation Act of 1973, a fair body of litigation had developed over the denial of testing accommodations for students with disabilities. Institutions are not required to modify the contents of exams or lower standards. Students with disabilities are expected to be held to the same academic standards. Students can be required to demonstrate that the requested modifications actually are related to disabilities.

Adult educational institutions should assess their technology and identify areas of inaccessibility, adopt a plan to address those areas, fully incorporate adaptive technology into their disability services programs, and involve necessary technology experts in meeting their obligations to reasonably accommodate. The U.S. Department of Justice and the Department of Education issued a joint letter on June 29, 2010, to all college and university presidents addressing the obligation to provide equal opportunity to technology and to ensure that use or adoption of emerging technology including access by students with disabilities (Salome Heyward and Associates, 2011). This letter followed a settlement agreement that the Department of Justice entered into with a number of institutions regarding their plan to use Kindle DX electronic book readers. This device was deemed not to have been fully accessible to students who were blind or had low vision. Therefore, it is no longer safe to assume that disparities in the level and degree of access provided to students with disabilities will go unchallenged. Institutions need to be proactive in planning and meeting the needs of students with disabilities.

Conclusion

For disability advocates, the change that the ADAAA has brought to the employment and educational environment was long overdue. The original Act was passed with an eye toward granting access to employment opportunities for those with disabilities. It was rooted in equity, fairness, and social justice. However, somehow the judiciary turned away from the original intent of the Act and allowed it to be narrowly construed. Effectively, the Act became oppressive, not liberating. The ADAAA clarifies the intent of Congress and makes it clear that the Act is now to be broadly read.

It is no longer difficult for employees or students to prove that they have a right to bring a claim of disability under the ADA or Section 504. Employers, especially, can no longer count on having disability claims defeated prior to going to trial. Before the 2009 amendments, much of the litigation in ADA cases involved questions about whether the employee was disabled. In these cases, courts frequently dismissed the claim in the employer's favor on summary judgment due to the stringent interpretations of the ADA's definition of disability. As a result of the ADAAA and its parallel revisions to Section 504 of the Rehabilitation Act of 1973, plaintiffs are more likely to clear the disability hurdle; therefore, we can expect to see much more litigation in the future focused on complex ADA issues regarding reasonable accommodations and undue hardship. A new day has dawned in the fight for social justice and equity for those with disabilities.

References

Albertsons Inc. v. Kirkingburg, 527 U.S. 555, 1999.
Americans with Disabilities Act Amendments Act of 2008, 42 U.S.C.A. § 12101 et seq.
ADA Amendments Act of 2008. www.access-board.gov/About/laws/ada-amendments
    .htm.
Association on Higher Education and Disability. Definition of disability. n.d. a.
    www.ahead.org/publications/alert/may-09#9.
Association on Higher Education and Disability. "Reasonable Accommodation." n.d. b.
    www.ahead.ie/employment_employers_reasonableaccommodation.
Business and Legal Resources. HR Daily Advisor. From the Editors: Expert Insight, 2011.
    www.blr.com/hrtips/ada?.
Catholic University of America, Office of General Counsel. "Summary of Federal Laws."
    June 15, 2011. http://counsel.cua.edu/fedlaw/Adas.cfm.
Cino, V. "Labor: ADAAA in the Courts. Counsel Commentary." October 11, 2010.
    www.insidecounsel.com/2010/10/11/adaaa-in-the-courts.

Colker, R. "The Americans with Disabilities Act: The First Decade of Enforcement." Ohio State University Distinguished Lecture. October 17, 2001. http://moritzlaw .osu.edu/faculty/colker/colkerlecture.pdf.

Culotta, R. "ADA Amendments Act Take Effect January 1, 2009." 2010. Frilot LLC. www.Frilot.com/PDF/ADA%20amendment%20Amendment%20ACT2%20-%20Renee%20Culotta.PDF.

Fisher & Phillips LLP. "Meet the New ADA: Massive Changes Ahead for Nation's Employers." September 18, 2008. www.laborlawyers.com/shownews.Aspx?Show= 10879&Type=1122.

Grizzell v. Cyber City Teleservices Marketing, Inc., 2010 (Middle District, Tenn., 2010).

Hoffman v. Carefirst of Fort Wayne, Inc., d/b/a Advanced Healthcare, 2010 WL 35225573 (N.D. Ind. 2010).

Jenkins v. National Board of Medical Examiners, 2009 U.S. App. LEXIS 2660. 2009 Fed. App. 0117N (6th Cir).

Kaloi, L. "Update on Section 504 and ADA," n.d. Ohio State University. http://principals office.osu.edu/files/landscape.9.09.php.

Kaloi, L., and Stanberry, K. "Section 504 in 2009: Broader Eligibility, More Accommodations." 2009. National Center for Learning Disabilities. www.ncld.org/on-capitol-hill/federal-laws-aamp-ld/adaaa-a-section504/section-504-in-2009.

McClure, M. "Plaintiffs Gain Momentum in New ADAAA Litigation." September 13, 2010. http://aremploymentlaw.com.

Murphy v. United Parcel Service, 527 U.S. 516 (1999).

National Center for Learning Disabilities. "Transitioning to College 2011." www.ncld.org/college-aamp-work/post-high-school-options/transitioning-to-college.

Rocco, T., and Fornes, S. "Perspectives on Disability in Adult and Continuing Education." In A. Rose, C. Kasworm, and J. Ross-Gordon (eds.), *The Handbook of Adult and Continuing Education*. Thousand Oaks, Calif.: Sage, 2010.

Salome Heyward and Associates. "It's Time to Adopt a Proactive Approach to Providing Access to Technology." www.salomeheyward.info/index.php.

Sample, J. *Avoiding Legal Liability: For Adult Educators, Human Resource Developers, and Instructional Designers*. Malabar, Fla.: Krieger Publishing, 2007.

Section 504 of the Rehabilitation Act of 1973, 29 U.S.C.A. § 794 et seq.

Sutton et al. v. United Air Lines, Inc., 527 U.S. 471, 1999.

Toyota Motor Manufacturing, Kentucky, Inc. v. Williams, 534 U.S. 184, 2002.

U.S. Equal Employment Opportunity Commission. "EEOC Files Trio of New Cases Under Amended Americans With Disabilities Act. [Press release]. September 9, 2010a. www1.eeoc.gov//eeoc/newsroom/release/9-9-10a.cfm?.

U.S. Equal Employment Opportunity Commission. "EEOC Sues Fisher, Collins, & Carter for Disability Discrimination." [Press release]. September 9, 2010b. www.eeoc.gov/eeoc/newsroom/release/9-9-10b.cfm.

Webber, D. *AIDS and the Law*, 4th ed. New York: Aspen Publishers, 2011.

W3C. "Web Content Accessibility Guidelines 2.0." December 11, 2008. www.w3.org/ TR/WCAG20/.

Zappe, J. "ADA Changes for 2009 Broaden Definition of Disability." December 31, 2008. www.ere.net/2008/12/31/.

LORENZO BOWMAN is a professor of business and management at DeVry University/Keller Graduate School of Management, Atlanta, Georgia, and is a member of the State Bar of Georgia.

10

Oppression of people with disabilities is subtle and often has a paternalistic subtext: Able-bodied people know what is best for the person with a disability.

Moving Forward: Two Paradigms and Takeaways

Tonette S. Rocco

Disability is not something one experiences in isolation of other characteristics. Sociocultural characteristics, such as race, class, gender, sexual orientation, age and disability, interact with each other in various combinations forming unique adults (Ross-Gordon, 2002). When interacting with other characteristics, disability can dominate the other characteristics—not because it is in some way more important but because disability is rarely seen as anything other than pathology, something to be pitied or cured. Disability is rarely understood in adult education as a socially constructed category or an identity marker used to oppress and categorize. Oppression of people with disabilities is subtle and often has a paternalistic subtext: Able-bodied people know what is best for the person with a disability. For instance, as I sat down to write this chapter, I heard in passing a news story about a young woman who is blind given an opportunity to ski. She explained that often she is told she can't do something because it is too dangerous, too difficult, too something; this time she was given an opportunity to learn to ski and did.

Clark (2006) suggested that disability studies and adult education should form an interdisciplinary relationship "as a way to investigate the disability experience within the adult learning context" (p. 308). She felt this relationship was necessary or important because in adult education, disability is viewed from a technical rational approach rather than a socially constructed perspective.

The technical rational approach involves the notion of fixing something by using instructional interventions or technologies to reach students who learn differently. "Differently" is a code word for those who do not learn in

NEW DIRECTIONS FOR ADULT AND CONTINUING EDUCATION, no. 132, Winter 2011 © 2011 Wiley Periodicals, Inc.
Published online in Wiley Online Library (wileyonlinelibrary.com) • DOI: 10.1002/ace.435

what is widely considered as the normal or dominant way. These instructional interventions and technologies were first viewed as undeserved special treatment for those with disabilities and have now reached the mainstream. Audiobooks and computers that read text out loud and have speech recognition functions were once expensive technologies designed to increase access to educational materials for people with disabilities. Now audiobooks are sold in stores, and the ability to read text and convert speech to text is standard on computers. Few nondisabled people who use these technologies know their history or the original market. However, I still hear from people with disabilities that they must get permission to digitally record a class as a form of accommodation when a person without a disability assumes the right to record the class and just does it. I hear from instructors that a student is "claiming" a disability and doesn't deserve the special treatment afforded to him or her because of legislation designed to protect the rights of the disabled. Instructors and students have a hard time seeing someone as having a disability if they can do things such as attend college.

Clark's (2006) suggestion that adult education and disability studies form a relationship has not been heeded by the field. The adult education scholars, whose work was informed by disability studies scholars prior to her essay, are the same ones doing this work now. The social construction of disability has been a main tenet of disability studies scholars since its inception in the early 1970s (Oliver, 1996). While the social construction of race, gender, and sexual orientation is a frequent theme in adult education, disability is still viewed from a technical rational perspective. Until this sourcebook, the closest the field came to viewing disability as socially constructed was Ross-Gordon's (2002) chapter exploring the sociocultural contexts for learning of adults with disabilities and her presentation of the intersection of disability with race, class, and gender. This sourcebook was conceptualized from a disability studies paradigm. Several of the chapters come from this paradigm, while others come from a more technical rational approach. It is important that both perspectives inform any discussion of disability in adult education.

Concepts from Disability Studies

Adult education has not joined with disability studies to trouble the concept of disability. Instead, disability is a taken-for-granted concept and experience. This critique of adult education is echoed in the chapters of this sourcebook. Several authors (Rocco and Delgado; McLean; Munger and Mertens; Walker; and Belzer and Ross-Gordon) describe the social construction of disability and implore adult educators to explore disability and its social construction. This social construction of disability is the reason for impairments. For instance, if all buildings were built with ramps and doorways and other spaces wide enough to accommodate wheelchairs, then

New Directions for Adult and Continuing Education • DOI: 10.1002/ace

people who use wheelchairs for mobility might not be thought of as disabled. People who wear eyeglasses are not considered disabled because less than perfect vision is easily accommodated.

In Chapter 1, Tonette S. Rocco and Antonio Delgado suggest that definitions are important to setting the boundaries for a term or concept. Sometimes these boundaries assist in creating a political presence to fight for liberation, and sometimes the boundaries aid in the categorization and oppression of people. An understanding of the definitions and how they are socially constructed is necessary in order to challenge them. Margaret A. McLean, in Chapter 2, observes that knowledge is socially constructed and what we know about people with disabilities can be challenged through experiencing disability and disabled people. Wayland Walker, in Chapter 5, challenges the social construction of multiple personalities or alters as a disorder or disability using as an example the classification of homosexuality as a mental illness in the early part of the twentieth century and declassified toward the end of the same century. In Chapter 3, Kelly M. Munger and Donna M. Mertens touch on the same issue with Deaf people who consider themselves members of a unique cultural group with their own language and traditions and not disabled.

The social construction of disability supports the privileged status of able-bodied people much in the same way the social construction of race supports white privilege. Privilege is generally unacknowledged and taken for granted by those who benefit from it. Racism stems from and supports white privilege just as ableism stems from the privileges enjoyed by the nondisabled or temporarily able-bodied population. Rocco and Delgado define ableism as a system of beliefs, processes, and practices used to support one human condition as normal and preferred and the other as not normal or desirable. McLean adds that this system creates barriers to full participation and citizenship for many disabled people. People with disabilities and disability studies scholars argue for a redefinition of disability that fosters human rights and social justice. Rocco and Delgado call for adult educators to consider disability a social justice concern. McLean, Munger, and Mertens and Belzer and Ross-Gordon call for adult educators to challenge the social construction of disability and to investigate disability using research methods that go beyond the traditional quantitative paradigm and instead use a transformative paradigm that honors social justice and human rights.

Concepts from the Technical Rational Perspective

The technical rational perspective is pragmatic. Concepts under this perspective include learning to cope with the disability, learning skills to mitigate the impact of the disability on one's life, and believing the disability is a private and individual or family concern rather than something imposed by society. In Chapter 4, Stephen Brookfield describes his learning journey

New Directions for Adult and Continuing Education • DOI: 10.1002/ace

to accept and find appropriate treatment for his depression. He charges adult educators and society with the task of assisting those with depression "to learn how to recognize, monitor, and cope with such depression, and requiring adult educators to provide education about this condition." In Chapter 6, Thomas G. Reio, Jr., and Sandra Fornes describe their learning journeys as parents of children with disabilities. While Brookfield initially tried to hide his depression and was overwhelmed by this effort, Reio and Fornes speak of feeling overwhelmed with trying to learn about their children's disabilities in a way that might help their children progress cognitively and physically.

In Chapter 7, Fariba Ostovary and Janet Dapprich present the issues and concerns of returning veterans and provide practical advice to adult educators on specific accommodations that might be warranted for veterans with posttraumatic stress syndrome. In Chapter 9, Lorenzo Bowman helps the reader understand what has changed in terms of the legal rights of people with disabilities since the Americans with Disabilities Act amendments were passed. He warns that employers will no longer have the upper hand when suits are filed claiming discrimination based on disability status.

Takeaways

We hope readers take away with them some principles, cautions, and suggestions after reading this sourcebook. Some key points from each chapter are:

- Adult educators should consider disability experience a social justice and human rights issue.
- Adult educators should foster relationship building and interactions between students with and without disabilities.
- Research should be conducted that furthers the social justice goals and human rights of people with disabilities in addition to considering the researcher's agenda.
- People diagnosed with cognitive, mental, and physical disorders can embark on self-directed learning projects to find the correct combination of medicine and treatments for themselves.
- Recognition of ableism, paternalism, sexism, and racist beliefs in oneself and how these beliefs might impede social justice work is an important step in working with people with disabilities in classrooms and workplaces.
- Parents can and should assist their children by finding ways for them to develop physically and cognitively despite the medical diagnosis.
- People with disabilities have a right to accommodations, and these accommodations simply level the field.

New Directions for Adult and Continuing Education • DOI: 10.1002/ace

References

Clark, M. "Adult Education and Disability Studies, an Interdisciplinary Relationship: Research Implication for Adult Education." *Adult Education Quarterly*, 2006, *56*(4), 308–322.

Oliver, M. *Understanding Disability from Theory to Practice*. New York: St. Martin's Press, 1996.

Ross-Gordon, J. M. "Sociocultural Contexts of Learning Among Adults with Disabilities." In M. V. Alfred (ed.), *Learning and Sociocultural Contexts: Implications for Adults, Community, and Workplace Education*. New Directions for Adult and Continuing Education, no. 96. San Francisco: Jossey-Bass, 2002.

TONETTE S. ROCCO is associate professor and graduate program director, Adult Education and Human Resource Development, Florida International University, Miami, Florida.

INDEX

Page references followed by *fig* indicate an illustrated figure.

OTHER TITLES AVAILABLE IN THE NEW DIRECTIONS FOR
ADULT AND CONTINUING EDUCATION SERIES
Susan Imel and Jovita M. Ross-Gordon, COEDITORS-IN-CHIEF

For a complete list of back issues, please visit www.josseybass.com/go/ndace

ACE131 Adult Education and the Pursuit of Wisdom

Elizabeth J. Tisdell, Ann L. Swartz

Times of change always feel complex, and today's world seems to
be changing constantly in more ways than we can track. Adult
educators working with adult learners desire deeply to act and
speak with wisdom that will offer a sense of truth and stability.
Further, as lifelong learners, most of us—educators and learners
both—are on a quest for wisdom. Indeed, who among us has never
wished for wisdom? Perhaps we wanted to do the right thing for
someone in trouble, or save a threatened relationship; perhaps we
sought wisdom as understood by the ancients, or wondered how
to follow a spiritual path in the light of a great wisdom tradition.
Maybe we just wanted to maximize our retirement plan so our
family would be cared for when we are gone. Adult education has
helped us to become more knowledgeable; perhaps it can also
expand our capacity for wisdom.

There is little available consideration of the meaning of wisdom in
the field of adult education. This volume explores the possibility of
educating for wisdom from multiple perspectives, through the insights
of several adult education practitioners who share their own experiences and call upon many bodies of literature. Hopefully, it not only
will contribute knowledge about wisdom itself, but also will facilitate
wise teaching and learning for and by adults.
ISBN: 978-1-1181-3327-9

ACE130 Adult Education for Health and Wellness

Lilian H. Hill

One task of adulthood is caring for one's health, and, for many,
caring for the health of children, a spouse or significant other, or
aging parents. Health changes over time in response to wellness
activities, aging, or disease. Adult learning is central to people's
abilities to cope with changing physical abilities, medical conditions, and the changes in lifestyle and social conditions resulting
from them. Chapters in this volume address:

- How adults learn while coping with chronic illness
- Curriculum design for a program for parents with special
  needs children
- Health education within adult literacy, adult basic education,
  and English as a Second Language classes
- Ways to address the needs of adults who have low levels of
  health literacy
- Means of increasing cultural competence among health
  workers to meet the needs of diverse patients
- Community education performed by trained indigenous
  community health advisors
- Approaches to help adults evaluate and learn from online
  information
- The influence of globalism on health
- Ways that health education can be a social justice issue

This diversity of arenas prompts new roles for adult educators. They provide health education alone or in collaboration with health professionals, and they educate health professionals about adults' learning needs, especially individuals who have low levels of health literacy and are from diverse cultural backgrounds. They create meaningful curricula, assist individuals to interpret health information, and influence the design of online information. Other important contributions include training local individuals to serve as community health advisors, helping adults cope with health challenges rooted in increasing globalism, and working for social justice. Finally, adult educators can work with communities to create health-related public policy that contributes to improved quality of life.

ISBN: 978-1-1180-8878-4

ACE129 Meeting Adult Learner Needs Through the Nontraditional Doctoral Degree

James P. Pappas, Jerry Jerman

As the world has grown more complex, so have the learning needs of adults who wish to be professionally and personally equipped for a continually changing global environment. Increasingly, so-called nontraditional students have sought additional educational opportunities and advanced credentials for intellectual growth, career advancement, or both. With demand for this highest level of credential increasing, institutions are rethinking their doctoral programs, and nontraditional doctoral programs have evolved to accommodate the needs of adult students. These programs combine academic rigor with applied knowledge, scholarship, convenience, and flexibility and come in a variety of formats. The colleges and universities—public and private, nonprofit and for-profit—that respond to this increasing market have discovered both a surprising number of committed students and a new revenue stream. This volume of *New Directions for Adult and Continuing Education* explores the emergence of the nontraditional doctoral degree, the characteristics of the nontraditional doctoral student, faculty concerns, program innovation, and unique programs at four institutions. Both scholars and practitioners will find it an interesting and engaging introduction to the topic.

ISBN: 978-1-1180-2763-9

ACE128 The Struggle for Democracy in Adult Education

Dianne Ramdeholl, Tania Giordani, Thomas Heaney, Wendy Yanow

Adult education in the United States has its roots in democracy. Early in the twentieth century, adult education was often described as a "movement," a spontaneous emergence of study circles, town hall meetings, and learning groups, all engaged in better understanding their world to build a better one democratically. Education in its broadest sense—learning to name the world—was at the center of that movement.

At the same time, and at the opposite end of the spectrum, were those who made the leap from lifelong learning to lifelong schooling. Collapse of the almost-movement was inevitable. Educators in the workplace and in formal institutions of learning sought to shape minds, rather than free them. Consequently, adult education grew up alongside a practice that devalued learning for democratic action and stressed adaptation to the workplace, corporate America, and a consumer economy.

Perhaps nostalgia is a lingering desire to return to a past that never was, but many adult educators, including the authors represented in this volume, have been attempting to reclaim their birthright—a critical but steadfast commitment to building democracy. In this book we build on the historic relationship between adult education and democracy. We examine an adult education practice that not only shapes minds, but also seeks to build communities of collaborative action. We explore best practices in shared and informed decision making within different contexts of adult education—in the community, the classroom, and the university—by focusing on various aspects of our work as adult education practitioners.
ISBN: 978-1-1180-0302-2

ACE127 **Adult Education in Cultural Institutions: Aquariums, Libraries, Museums, Parks, and Zoos**
Edward W. Taylor, Marilyn McKinley Parrish
On any given week millions of adults around the world can be found gathering in libraries, parks, zoos, arboretums, and museums in person or online. These cultural institutions are seen as repositories of knowledge and collections of a community's cultural or natural heritage. However, they are much more. They are structures that promote cognitive change: commons, places of community outside of home and work, where individuals and groups gather to share and discuss ideas. Cultural institutions may be sites of conflict and contestation where economic and political challenges call into question institutional purpose and mission, and debates emerge over whose story is told. They can also serve as sites of deliberative democracy that foster social change and reform, where community members can engage with challenging and important societal issues. This volume aims to forge a stronger relationship between adult educators and educators within cultural institutions in an effort to better understand adult learning and teaching within these sites of nonformal education and the role these institutions play in society.
ISBN: 978-0-4709-5208-5

ACE126 **Narrative Perspectives on Adult Education**
Marsha Rossiter, M. Carolyn Clark
This volume presents a variety of perspectives on the role of narrative in adult learning and explores how those perspectives can be translated into practice. Interest in narrative among adult educators has been a continuing strand of our professional dialogue for some time, and it continues to grow as we become increasingly appreciative of the multifaceted views of adult learning that are revealed through the narrative lens. The range of narrative applications, implications, and perspectives in adult education is practically limitless. The perspectives included in this sourcebook, while not an exhaustive review, do convey something of the rich variety and scope a narrative approach offers adult learning.
ISBN: 978-0-4708-7465-3

ACE125 **White Privilege and Racism: Perceptions and Actions**
Carole L. Lund, Scipio A. J. Colin, III
White privilege is viewed by many as a birthright and is in essence an existentialist norm that is based upon the power and privilege of pigmentation. Because it is the norm for the white race, this privilege is virtually invisible, but its racist byproducts are not. It becomes

common for whites to believe falsely that their privilege was earned by hard work and intellectual superiority; it becomes the center of their worldview. The reality is that when they defend their pigmentary privilege, what they are really saying is that peoples of color have earned their disadvantage. Unless whites recognize this privilege and the consequent racist attitudes and behaviors, they will continue to perpetuate racism in both their personal and professional lives. It is their responsibility to commit to a significant paradigm shift by recognizing their privilege, critiquing the impact on peoples of color, and making the decision to reconfigure their attitudes and alter their behaviors. This volume focuses on facilitating our understanding of the conceptual correlation between white privilege and racism and how these intertwined threads are manifested in selected areas of adult and continuing education practice. Although there seems to be a consensus that this practice reflects sociocultural and intellectual racism, there has been no discussion of linkages between the white racist ideology, white privilege, and white attitudes and behaviors behind that racism.
ISBN: 978-0-4706-3162-1

ACE124 **Reaching Out Across the Border: Canadian Perspectives in Adult Education**
Patricia Cranton, Leona M. English
This volume brings together Canadian scholars and practitioners to articulate a variety of historical, geographical, and political positions on the field of adult education in Canada. The chapter authors examine the country's interests and discourses and detail Canada's history, educational initiatives, movements, and linguistic struggles. Specifically, the authors address the uniqueness of Canada's emphasis on linking health and adult literacy; the use of video and dialogue to promote adult and literacy education in the North; the historical adult education initiatives such as Frontier College and the Antigonish movement; the special language and cultural issues that define Quebec's role of adult education and training; the development of critical adult education discourse in Canada; the emphasis on environmental adult education; the uniqueness of the community college system; and initiatives in adult education for community development. By describing Canadian accomplishments and lessons learned in adult education, this volume will help inform the practice, research, and studies of adult educators in the United States.
ISBN: 978-0-4705-9259-5